SOUTH BIRMINGHAM C

043046

D0280355

Tough _____ pping

SOUTH & CITY COLLEGE BIRMINGHAM
LIBRARY SERVICE
Digbeth Campus
Tel:**0121 694 5065**

Book No:	$O\,43046$

This book is due for return on or before the last date shown below:-

the Institute of Management

FOUNDATION

PITMAN
PUBLISHING

London · Hong Kong · Johannesburg · Melbourne
Singapore · Washington DC

The Institute of Management (IM) is at the forefront of management development and best management practice. The Institute embraces all levels of management from students to chief executives. It provides a unique portfolio of services for all managers, enabling them to develop skills and achieve management excellence.

If you would like to hear more about the benefits of membership, please write to Department P, Institute of Management, Cottingham Road, Corby NN17 1TT.

This series is commissioned by the Institute of Management Foundation.

PITMAN PUBLISHING
128 Long Acre, London WC2E 9AN

A Division of Pearson Professional Limited

First published in Great Britain 1996

© David Martin 1996

British Library Cataloguing in Publication Data
A CIP catalogue record for this book can be obtained from the British Library.

ISBN 0 273 62312 5

All rights reserved; no part of this publication may be reproduced, stored in a retrieval system, or transmitted in any form or by any means, electronic, mechanical, photocopying, recording, or otherwise without either the prior written permission of the Publishers or a licence permitting restricted copying in the United Kingdom issued by the Copyright Licensing Agency Ltd, 90 Tottenham Court Road, London W1P 9HE. This book may not be lent, resold, hired out or otherwise disposed of by way of trade in any form of binding or cover other than that in which it is published, without the prior consent of the Publishers.

10 9 8 7 6 5 4 3 2 1

Typeset by Pantek Arts, Maidstone, Kent
Printed and bound in Great Britain by Bell and Bain Ltd, Glasgow

The Publishers' policy is to use paper manufactured from sustainable forests.

Contents

■　■　■

The Author

David M. Martin FCIS, FIPD, FCB is a proven expert in the field of communications and has run his own business consultancy since 1985, carrying out various projects including corporate internal communications and personnel coaching and development. Before this he had 10 years' experience as a Director and Secretary of a listed PLC.

He is a regular speaker at seminars and author of bestselling business titles: *Tough Talking, Dealing with Demanding Customers, Manipulating Meetings* and *How to be a Great Communicator*.

He is also a consultant editor of Business Administration.

SOUTH BIRMINGHAM COLLEGE

651·73 MAR

043046.

LIBRARY HALL GREEN

19|4|96

Introduction

■ ■ ■

The following are the general themes of a number of books which I have written loosely based on the need for the effective two-way dialogue that is real communication:

1 communication is often falsely assumed when it is information (a one-way dissemination of data) that is actually occurring;

2 in seeking to attain two-way communication, we need to establish our desired result, rather than, as often seems to be the case, scoring debating points (the effect of which may actually be to distance ourselves from that desired result), and

3 before every interface we need to prepare rather than trying to 'think on our feet'.

There is nothing particularly original about these points, which makes the fact that many fail to observe them all the more surprising.

This book's forerunners, *Tough Talking*, and its sequels, *Manipulating Meetings* and, to a lesser extent, *Dealing with Demanding Customers*, concentrated on face to face interchanges rather than with interchanges over the telephone, and as such posed far less difficult problems. Telephone interchanges consist of remote and distance interfacing (the two parties not being face to face) which adds considerably to the communication difficulties. If it is important that we prepare for a face to face confrontation, then this is absolutely vital when we contemplate a confrontation over the telephone. Not only will we not be able to provide a large amount of what we feel by our body language, but also we will not be able to perceive a large amount of what the other party feels because we cannot see *their* body language.

Body language can account for between 40 and 50 per cent of the understanding of the messages that pass, whilst American research indicates that during a telephone call, the recipient may recall as little as 11 per cent of the message. With these kinds of barriers to comprehension it should hardly need saying that, marvellous invention though the telephone is, its use should be treated with far more respect and preparation than is often the case. Indeed the familiarity, convenience and speed of the device may have bred both contempt and a lack of awareness that, if we are to be successful telephone communicators (which personal conceit may well lead us to assume we are), then we do need to prepare for every call to a far greater extent than we often do.

Experience and research indicates that most users actually fail this basic requirement, and that this is particularly true when dealing with the more difficult calls. As a result, such calls may either end in failure or require explanatory follow up, or lead to aggravation and further calls, correspondence or meetings. If this occurs then not only has the call itself failed but also we will create wasteful situations which could so easily have been avoided by greater preparation as well as an appreciation of 'where the other party was coming from'.

Thus the purpose of *Tough Telephoning* is:

- to explore the steps we should be taking before making a call, and suggest ways in which we can make it easier for ourselves to achieve successful calls

- to demonstrate the barriers to communication that exist in using the phone and to show how these can be removed, at least in part, by preparation for, and consideration of, the task; and

- above all, to provide guidance on the many tactics and approaches that will help make our calls more efficient, purposeful and effective.

In short the book seeks to help us get what we want from a call and in many ways, since if you can avoid a confrontation (even if such avoidance carries a minor cost or inconvenience) you may still be a winner, also seeks to show, with relatively little extra effort, how to avoid the worst of 'tough telephoning'.

David M. Martin
Buddenbrook
February 1996

It's good to talk

Key learning points

1 Since the use of the telephone is expanding rapidly and is due to expand still more rapidly (particularly with the rapid development of e-mail) as users we need to pay careful attention to the way that we use the medium.

2 The device is one of the communication marvels of our lifetime but we need to ensure our preparation and verbal skills are equal to the challenge and opportunities it presents.

3 Too often we use the phone casually, without preparation and also confuse information and communication. The terms are not inter-substitutional and we need to assess which is which.

4 When making (or taking) a call we are geographically remote from the other party which means we are remote in every way in communication terms – such remoteness does not aid true communication and we must allow for this 'communication filter'.

5 Various obstructions exist between us and our target which can be very effective in creating barriers and helping create tough calls, so ways of offsetting the problems they create need to be implemented.

Thank you Mr Bell

■ ■ ■

There it sits foursquare on our desks, courtesy of the inventive minds of the so appropriately-named American inventor Alexander Graham Bell using electromagnetism first developed by the English inventor Michael Faraday – the telephone. It is perhaps appropriate that it took a combination of the thoughts of the sons of two great nations to invent a device which, amongst many other uses, helps bridge the 4,000 miles of ocean between them. It is not just the ocean that separates us, as the Americans and the British are said to be 'two nations separated by a common language'.

In considering the problems posed by our use of Bell and Faraday's marvellous invention, it may be appropriate to rework this old jibe and define a telephone call as being a device for communication made between two persons separated by mutual misconceptions and individual prejudices. Actually it is incorrect to describe Bell as an American as he was a Scot from Edinburgh who did not become an American until 1882 – six years after he had invented the telephone – by which time he had sold all his rights to it. It is not even accurate to say Bell invented the 'telephone' as the term had previously been applied to a number of inventions during the 50 years prior to his invention.

Misconceptions seem to abound in relation to the telephone. Before we consider others related to this invention which are often the root cause of a considerable number of our tough business calls (many of which, as we shall see, we actually bring upon ourselves) let us first place the invention itself in context, particularly as its use is expanding at a phenomenal rate, posing problems in their own right.

Indeed, it may be that it is the development of the technology which is the root cause of some of these problems – the seeds of the problems and disputes may lie in the very success of

2

the acceptance of telephone technology. Many of us tend to treat our use of the phone in a very casual, instinctive manner. It is all too easy – telephonic communication has become a service where human input (other than that of the caller and respondent) has been virtually eliminated. If we are not careful the machine may come to rule our lives – if, indeed, it does not already do so.

Case study 1.1
'LA DAMN BELL SANS MERCI HATH THEE IN THRALL'

Imagine you are deep in thought regarding a problem, or in a confidential meeting or interview. The office door may be closed giving a sign to all-comers that you have no wish to be disturbed. Should anyone have the temerity to knock and open the door they will normally have the courtesy to ask if it is convenient to interrupt (or possibly ask for an indication of how long it will be before you can give their problem some attention). No such niceties exist for the telephone caller. The strident ring of its bell ('la damn bell' of the title to misquote Keats) imperiously summons us, and, in order to get some peace, we answer it immediately. Regardless of whether we take the call or not, our attention is distracted, the train of thought broken. Is it any surprise that under such circumstances we may sometimes react instinctively and negatively against the caller and that this instant reaction may create a tough call where none previously existed or was necessary? Such interruption can cause irritation which may surface in our subsequent dealing with what may otherwise be innocuous. In *10 Minutes Time and Stress Management* (Piatkus, 1995) Dr David Lewis refers to a study which showed that the average manager is interrupted every eight minutes and once interrupted it takes several minutes to recover their previous working efficiency. He points out that one of the most common causes of interruptions is the telephone.

3

Never mind the content – feel the quality (of the connection)
■ ■ ■

Of course there are ways of defeating the interruption outlined in Case Study 1.1 – even, these days, being able to discover the telephone number of the caller thus allowing us 'not to be there' if we do not want to talk to them. The latest versions of Bell's original cumbersome prototype are virtually mini-computers in their own right. They are superb examples of marvellous devices that are simultaneously one of the greatest benefits to business and possibly potentially one of its greatest curses. They provide us with the means, courtesy of another American – Thomas Edison who invented the original telephone exchange – by which we can almost instantly convey our every thought (worthy or otherwise) virtually anywhere within the world. Unfortunately, the giddy delusions of power that consideration of this point may create should be instantly tempered by the realisation that the self-same tiny implement is also the means by which anyone in the world can convey their every thought (similarly worthy or otherwise, welcome or not, timely or intrusive) to us – regardless of whether or not we want them to do so.

4

Case study 1.2

DERAILING THE TRAIN OF THOUGHT

The first chapter of any book is probably the most difficult to write. Whilst drafting this one in leafy (and dripping wet) Epping, England, the telephone rang and my train of thought was derailed by someone calling from Botswana who had read an article I had written and wanted more information. The caller was speaking from the edge of the Kalahari desert and virtually on the Tropic of Capricorn – the connection was as clear as a bell - and so was his request with which I dealt speedily, and equally speedily returned to the throes of composition. However, inspiration had dried up and the thread was broken – but it did provide a timely example of the problem of the telephone being the thought interrupter *par excellence* and the potential generator of irritation leading to tough calls.

Global connections
■ ■ ■

Botswana is in a different global hemisphere and thousands of miles from Essex and yet within seconds of my caller reading an article he had connected with the writer, truly the world is rapidly shrinking. We have to be prepared for an increasing number of such calls – and from people whose culture, language and comprehension may be very different to our own – thus almost inevitably creating tough calls. The technology may achieve an almost miraculous telephonic connection but as mere humans our challenge is to manage the cerebral connection effectively.

Case study 1.3

IT'S A KNOCKOUT

The UK subsidiary of an American publisher was celebrating the launch of its 500th book with a party and 'knockout' competition at a local hotel during working hours. To ensure contact could be maintained the telephone number of the hotel had been left with the American parent. However, no-one had warned the new young switchboard operator at the hotel and when she found herself speaking to the president of the American parent she quite literally froze, thinking she was speaking to THE American president! In her confusion she cut the connection. The Americans were not best pleased at having to ring again.

5

Key technique

Too often we place people entirely lacking in experience and training in difficult situations where, faced with something alien to them, they are at a loss as to what to do. This is not the fault of the person – but of the organisation – on which it cannot do otherwise than reflect badly, probably creating a tough call as well.

Portability and penetration
■ ■ ■

In fact, of course, I am not being entirely precise by referring to the devices as sitting foursquare on our desks since nowadays the development of lightweight even colourful portable phones means that the latest offspring of the original heavy black handsets can accompany us everywhere. They may indeed be residing in our jacket pocket or handbag wherever we may be reading this book – on tube, aircraft – even in the loo! No matter where we are, or why we are there, we now need never be out of telephone contact again. Many enthusiasts claim this as a major step forward, others (perhaps including several members of the British Royal Family and at least one American president) may regard it as very much a mixed blessing. In Japan recently, consumers have been able to buy a personal handiphone system (PHS) which not only provides cheap and instant sound communication within a fairly limited radius (the diameter of its reception area is only up to 500 metres, although apparently this will be sufficient for it to answer the needs of 50 per cent of Japan's cramped population) but it also has an existing capacity to carry moving pictures which might make the portable videophone concept imminent. Japan's population apparently cannot get enough phones. They already have over four million subscribers to portable phones, despite the penetration of such devices having been severely restricted by State regulation until April 1994.

As far as the United Kingdom is concerned the telephone has gained 91 per cent penetration of the population. Thus only 9 per cent of the entire population do not have, or have immediate access to, a phone, whilst presumably fewer still have not used or are unused to using them. Furthermore, the above reference to portable phones should scarcely be reduced to an afterthought, since according to the *Financial Times* newsletter there were 16.3 million cellular phone subscribers in western Europe on 1st May 1995, an increase of 61 per cent on the figure for the previous year. In America it is estimated that no less than 1 in 10 of the population has a cellular phone, there they have a massive 25 million subscribers. That country's portable phone industry customer base has doubled in two years and new customers are still being added at a rate of 28,000 each day. Perhaps this is hardly surprising as 93 per cent of US homes have telephones, 70 per cent have two phones and on average each household makes over 3,500 calls per year – almost ten a day!

The appeal of always being in telephone contact, as well as the flexibility of the new phones, are helping to expand the market at a very rapid pace and inevitably this potential market is attracting increasing numbers of new manufacturers and considerable capital investment which, in turn, is leading to constant improvements in both the performance of the machines and in their versatility. The array of 'add-ons' is considerable and growing.

Clear reception
■ ■ ■

Whilst this increasing sophistication and flexibility must be welcomed, what appears to be constantly overlooked in all this is the human dimension. There is a great danger in becoming so dazzled by the technology that we forget the original purpose – allowing one person remote from another to speak to that person – and, above all to make themselves understood to them.

Despite the immense range of telecommunication equipment and its increasing sophistication, at the end of the day the purpose of the phone is very simple – to allow one human being to communicate with another. The problem is that in considering the beauty, capabilities and potential of the equipment we tend to overlook the fact that to the unwary and the unthinking the telephone is actually anything but an ideal medium for the purpose for which it was intended, that of conversation and communication, other than for routine confirmation of factual matters. The suggested range of ideal uses (see later) is actually quite short. In reality, circumstances force us to use the telephone for a variety of purposes including some for which it may be anything but ideal. Whilst we could achieve success were we to think about the use and prepare adequately for it, since often we do not, it is hardly surprising if we find that a fair proportion of our calls end up being tough.

American research indicates that as little as 11 per cent of a message or information that a caller wishes to convey to a respondent is actually retained by the respondent after a telephone call. If, instead, a letter, fax or e-mail message (see Chapter Thirteen) is sent, which is then in turn followed by a telephone conversation then what we might call this 'receptivity factor' rises to around 25 per cent. Obviously this is a considerable improvement but it is still a long way from the 60–70 per cent plus figure that will normally be achieved should the two parties meet and discuss matters face to face. It is essential when considering our use of the telephone that we recognise the barriers that are present in using the device as a medium for communication. In face to face conversation as much as 40–50 per cent of the message will be conveyed by our body language. We will probably be unaware of most of the messages that we send by our own body language although we will subconsciously be aware of that of the other party to the encounter.

8

Communication obstructions
■ ■ ■

The effectiveness of all means of communication is reduced by obstructions that exist between (or can be deliberately erected by) one or both the parties. In using the phone we normally achieve only about a sixth of the effectiveness of the interface that we would achieve were we face to face. Why should this be so? The basic problem, which affects all interfacing, whether written, visual or verbal is that we often confuse what is essentially the dissemination of information (ie a one-way traffic flow) with communication (which is essentially two-way). My caller from Botswana rang to say he wanted to obtain an item to which I had referred in an article. That is a request for information. We did not start to communicate until he outlined his problems and I then asked some questions to which he provided the answers and thus more information.

Similarly, if I pick up my phone to call a colleague to arrange a meeting (one ideal use of the phone), that is information. But we do not start to communicate until my colleague says 'Sorry,

Sender			
Data encoded	I		C
Transmitted	N	F	O
Received	F	E	M
Decoded	O	E	M
	R	D	U
	M	B	N
Recipient	A	A	I
Received	T	C	C
Decoded	I	K	A
Comprehension	O		T
Clarification	N		I
			O
			N

Figure 1.1 Information is not communication

(from the author's *How to be a Great Communicator*)

can't make Wednesday – could make it Thursday – can you do that?' Again, if a manager phones a teleworker (one of the growth sectors of employment we shall consider later) and states that he needs the work that the teleworker has been allocated completed by Friday week, he may feel that he is communicating with his employee and will often describe the act as such. In fact, he is doing no such thing. In both cases the original call was information only. You could describe the manager's comment as an instruction although it does also provide information for the teleworker. But what if the teleworker is suffering from flu, her computer has developed a similar bug and her printer is also faulty? Unless this information is in turn relayed to the manager, the information that his worker cannot comply with his instruction will not be known. Communication, as the above illustration demonstrates, only occurs when we as the instigator of the call, get feedback from our target or respondent and start a **dialogue** with them.

The dual carriageway
∎ ∎ ∎

Communication is all about comprehension or understanding of each other's views. It requires a dialogue and the word dialogue should provide a clue to the essential two-way nature of the matter. Dialogue comes from the Greek - *'dia'* meaning 'with each other', and *'legein'* meaning 'speak'. The word came into English via French where it meant 'conversation, discussion or debate' (*Bloomsbury Dictionary of Word Origins*). Thus 'communication' is essentially about the factor 'two' – indeed it is fascinating to consider that the word itself contains two 'Cs', two 'Os', two 'Ms', two 'Is' and two 'Ns'. It is a very 'dually' orientated word, and so should its use be. Yet often, and particularly in UK business where we tend not to be good communicators (although many delude themselves that they are, which simply compounds the problem), we see a process of information provision described as communication. It is perhaps not surprising if problems then arise.

If this quite widespread misconception were not bad enough, there are other basic problems which affect all communications between people but specifically phone calls. These further difficulties are set out below.

Obstructions to communication
■ ■ ■

Physical obstructions

1 *The fact that the respondent is deep in thought about some other matter and, resenting being dragged away from consideration of it, gives only part of their attention to the message.*

Case study 1.4

THE 'DOUBLE-GLAZING' SCENARIO

The Director was up to her eyes in work when the phone rang and her secretary announced that one of her advisers was on the line. Without thinking, the Director retorted 'and I suppose I'm supposed to listen to him ramble on for half an hour when I'm supposed to be preparing for the Board meeting' Nevertheless she took the call and was somewhat perplexed to discover that the call was completed very quickly although the adviser seemed a little aloof. Later her secretary admitted that she thought the interrupt device which would have prevented the caller hearing what was said whilst the call was being put through, had not been working and almost certainly the Director's instinctive reaction had been heard by the caller.

Key technique

Whilst potentially embarrassing, nevertheless the Director had albeit unwittingly, dealt with a problem that had been bothering her for some time – how to reduce the time spent being polite to the loquacious. Perhaps finding a way of conveying this view might assist in such a situation.

Warning: Don't assume that the other party cannot hear what you are saying, even if you cover the mouthpiece. This can also apply at the end of conversations if you do not firmly replace the receiver immediately. It should not be overlooked that covering the mouthpiece (which is usually discernible by the other party) could be considered very rude by them. It might be better to say 'would you excuse me for a moment' to deal with the matter.

Note: I have described this kind of call as 'double-glazing' as it emulates the unsolicited, unwanted and unhelpful calls so frequently made by representatives of that industry. However, at least the adviser's comments had some value which such calls normally do not and should be treated accordingly (see Chapters Ten and Eleven).

2 *The fact that the connection is poor and so it is difficult to understand what is being said.*

Whilst this is a rare occurrence these days on 'fixed' phones it is still a problem with portables. If the call is important but we cannot understand what is being said we may become angry and vent our spleen not on the phone but on the caller. Any such 'aggro' may generate a similar 'aggro' in response – a tough call can thus be created.

3 *The fact that the call is being taken in difficult surround-
ings e.g. within a very noisy environment (which may
again make it difficult to hear and/or concentrate).*

4 *The fact that the call (which is perhaps on a sensitive or
private matter) is being received in a situation where the
recipient does not want to 'let on' either about the subject or
the caller (or both).*

Case study 1.5

GET OUT OF THAT ONE

The executive had, unknown to his employer, applied for another position, and, somewhat unwisely, had provided the recruitment consultants
with his office number. During a conversation with his director, his internal
phone rang and he answered it. Whilst dealing with that call, his external
phone rang and the director answered it for him. To the executive's horror
he realised the call was from the consultant. He cut off his internal caller
and almost grabbed the phone from his boss's hand.

Key technique

Although 'power play' invites those susceptible to such images to
have more than one phone on their desk – no-one can effectively
communicate on two instruments simultaneously. (Indeed some of us
have problems on one!) Combined systems are more likely to be
cost-effective as well as helping to avoid embarrassing scenarios such
as the above.

Note: For those intrigued about the outcome . . . he thought quickly and
told his boss he had contacted the consultancy as he had heard that they
had recently conducted a survey on executive salaries and benefits in
which he was interested!

Key technique

The ability to think quickly (as well as laterally or innovatively) is often
essential in dealing with tough calls.

5 *The fact that the call is taken in a situation where there are distractions, for example, a busy office or one with plenty of glass, can cause the attention of the respondent to wander.*

6 *The fact that the call is taken when you are in the middle of something which can be continued during the call.*

This has at least two drawbacks

a the work may suddenly catch more of your attention so that attention to the content of the phone conversation is distracted and

b the caller can realise that they do not have all your attention and can feel somewhat miffed as a result.

Psychological obstructions

1 *The inconvenience of the message being received at a particular time (the respondent is thinking of what else (s)he should be doing and fails to concentrate on the message).*

2 *The antipathy felt towards the caller or message bearer that prevents the actual message getting through.*

13

Case study 1.6

NOT WHAT WAS SAID

The caller was trying to buy an air ticket by phone and kept dialling the number provided by the airline. After dialling he became increasingly frustrated by 'hearing' the recorded British Telecom (BT) announcement advising him to insert a '1' after the initial zero.

What was annoying him was the fact that, since when making many previous calls he had heard the recorded voice reminding him to 'insert a 1', he had now trained himself to do so automatically.

Eventually a colleague took the phone, dialled the number inserting the '1' and listened to the message. Far from advising the caller to insert a '1' the message actually told him to remove it and (effectively) dial the number he had originally been given which was correct after all. He did and was put straight through.

> **Key technique**
>
> We need to train ourselves to *listen* to the message being conveyed not the one that we think is being conveyed

Note: It might have been helpful had BT used a different voice (even a male rather than female voice) which itself would draw the attention of the caller to the fact that it was a different message to the standard one advising the caller to insert a '1', the content of which had become boring and 'not heard' through repetition. Similarly, changing the message on answerphones from time to time may encourage attention to the actual content.

---

3 *Unwillingness to accept what is being said. If the message is so at variance to expectations or contrary to preconceptions that the respondent may not be able to accept it at all.*

> **Case study 1.7**
>
> **A DEAD END JOB**

In ancient times when rulers tended to wield absolute power, it was quite common, should a messenger bring bad news (for example that a battle had been lost) for the poor chap to be executed simply for being the bearer of the tidings for which he had no responsibility whatever.

> **Key technique**
>
> Whilst it may be an ideal way of venting one's frustration (although not doing a great deal for the recruitment of messengers) executing the messenger (or, in modern times, losing one's temper) does not help the recipient understand the message one little bit.

Note: Conversely those messengers that brought good news could find themselves bountifully rewarded and one is tempted to wonder if ever bad news became translated to good by a messenger who took the gifts and quietly disappeared. It would say a great deal for their life expectancy if little for the accuracy of the communication. The point is that for a number of reasons the real message may not always get through.

4 *Unwillingness to accept the speed at which we may feel we are being pushed by the caller using the phone rather than writing.*

We might prefer to gain some time to reflect on the matter.

Language and comprehension obstructions

1 *The fact that one party insists on using language or jargon which the other does not wholly understand.*

Jargon can be said to be:

- the refuge of the insecure (since the underlying message is that 'I need to protect my position by using terms which only the privileged few will understand');

15

- the device of the lazy (since the user cannot be bothered to put the message in a form which can be understood by the recipient, not realising that if the respondent does not understand, it is the originator's fault); as well as

- the response of the patronising since another underlying message is – 'If you don't understand this why are you bothering to read or listen to it?' – which begs the question of the composer 'If you didn't mean it to be understood why did you bother to compose it?').

2 *The fact that the respondent may have listening difficulties which prevent absorption of the message.*

It should not be overlooked that some people are not good communicators and/or find difficulty in expressing themselves clearly.

3 *The fact that a caller may not actually understand the message he or she has been asked to convey.*

Case study 1.8
SAVING FACE

The administrative arrangements for conferences and seminars are often made by efficient secretaries who, excellent at their own job, cannot be expected to know and understand all the subject matter. The lecturer was phoned by her contact at the conference organisers and asked to add an item to the course she was giving. Not understanding what was being required she jotted down what she thought was being requested and agreed to insert the item. After the conference several of the delegate's critics queried why this matter had been inserted as it seemed to bear no relation to the rest of the presentation

16

Key technique

As well as trying to preserve the 'face' of the caller where it becomes obvious that they do not actually know what they are talking about, it is essential to record what one thinks has been asked for in writing with a request to confirm. It may still be wrong but at least the paper-work will demonstrate that you tried and may save a future tough call!

Acceptance obstructions

1 *Resentment at having to discuss the matter with the caller or communicator.*

Case study 1.9
NEVER MIND THE REASON

The member was of independent spirit and resented the position of the person who was in titular control. A request to ensure her attendance earlier than strictly necessary brought forth an instant retort 'that's b****y high-handed, who do you think you are' leading to a stand-up exchange and a heated row which resulted in the termination of the appointed member's contract. The basis of the original request was in order to help the administrative staff who were unable to cope with the rush caused by late-comers but this acceptable reason was never noted.

Key technique

Making false assumptions is one of the most frequent reasons for faulty communication. 'Don't assume – find out' is worthy advice.

2 *Resentment that the person giving the news is already in possession of it and therefore in a position of 'power'.*

Communication is difficult at the best of times, but with this array of difficulties we should not be surprised if a proportion of our calls turn out to be tough.

17

2

■ ■ ■

Let your fingers do the walking

Key learning points

1 There is a rising scale of communication – and unfortunately communication *via* the telephone is at a low point on
this scale. We must be prepared to counter this problem.

2 Lacking body language the content of our telephone conversation can be misinterpreted – less than 11 per cent of
the message may actually get through – we need to adjust
our approach accordingly.

3 We must create sufficient thinking time before we move
to calling time – in short to train ourselves to think before
we dial.

4 We also need to consider the various types of call and consider whether the telephone call is the best format for our
message, and/or whether we can improve our chances of
avoiding tough calls by augmenting its performance (and
our own) by using other means of communication.

Through the looking glass
■ ■ ■

In Chapter One several situations were identified which mitigate against our message actually getting through. Often these were viewed from the perspective of the respondent but we must not overlook that the situations can equally apply when we are the initiator of the call. We need to take to heart lessons similar to those highlighted under each heading 'key techniques' when we are the initiators of the call as much as when we are the recipients. Thus in Case Study 1.8, it might have been politic for the speaker not to let on that she thought the caller did not know what she was talking about in order to save face. However, viewed from the dimension of the conference organiser, it would have been more sensible to have said as her opening gambit 'Look, Hilary, my Director wants to add an item to the conference programme in your session and has asked me to ask you if you can cover 'certain statue rights' (actually what was required was a piece on 'asserting statutory rights') but I am not sure I understand what this means – does it ring any bells with you?' Trying to cover up an inadequacy of knowledge helps neither party – it may backfire on the perpetrator and certainly can only add to the confusion of the respondent.

20

Case study 2.1

NOT SUCH A DUSTY JOB

The Chairman of one of the Industrial Tribunals on which I sit told me that his three-year-old son had been asked what his father did. 'Daddy cleans,' replied his son proudly. 'Cleans – what do you mean – what does he clean?'

'He dusts bunals' came the confident reply.

Key technique

Misunderstanding is understandable in a child – indeed it can be endearing. In an adult, however, it totally lacks such appeal. Because we are adult we may not wish to admit we do not understand, but it may be dangerous to bluff it out. Saying we do not understand and asking for clarification protects our position. Bluffing can backfire and land us in all sorts of trouble.

The rising scale of communication
■ ■ ■

When we communicate with others remotely (whether on the phone, using e-mail, etc.) we make assumptions. This can be very serious – we should never assume as many assumptions turn out to be false (in any event in the words of the old saying 'assume' makes an 'ass' of 'u' and 'me'). The advice 'don't assume – find out' should be our guiding watchword. However, in many instances we do tend to assume that the respondent will, if they hear our message, understand its content in the same way that we understand it and mean it to be understood. Even if we avoid the difficulties of reaction highlighted by the obstructions set out in Chapter One we have other problems to contend with. Telephone conversation is remote communication based on sound alone. Research indicates that such 'sound alone' communication is one of the less effective means in terms of message retention and the various aspects of the following analysis of the 'scale of communication' bears study.

1 *If it is written communication* (for example: letters, reports, memos, articles, etc.) and (s)he does not make any notes, the average reader will remember of what (s)he reads   ... *about 10%*

2 *If it is audible communication* (for example: formal voice only presentation with no opportunity to ask questions,

etc.) the average listener will remember of what (s)he hears ... *about 20%*

Case study 2.2

SENT TO COVENTRY

Whilst researching this book I visited Birmingham. On the motorway just as I passed the junction leading to Coventry, I heard a speaker on the radio refer to Coventry as being in the top left hand corner of England which I would have thought started about 200 miles north of Coventry – say from above Liverpool to Carlisle. I was tempted to ring the pro- gramme and point out the error but was beaten to it by another caller who did ring in and stated that 'Rugby was in the Midlands, not in the top left hand corner of England'. Rugby and Coventry may be not that far apart geographically but the words are totally dissimilar.

Key technique

We do not always hear perfectly what is said and need to train our- selves to concentrate on what is being said (as well as what is not said) – particularly on the phone.

3 *If it is visual communication* (for example, picture-only video, silent demonstration, etc.) the viewer will remem- ber what percentage of what (s)he sees ... *about 30%*

4 *If it is communication which uses both visual and audible means* (for example television, commentary video, presen- tation with audio-visual aids, etc.) the viewer should remember what percentage of what (s)he sees and hears ... *about 50%*

Case study 2.3

CHECKING IT OUT

During several seminars on communication skills in 1995 I read a short passage to around 150 delegates. We then asked 12 questions on the sub- ject matter. Of the total who heard the passage six delegates scored 9, six scored 7 or 8 and the remainder scored 6 or less. Thus, the overwhelming number of delegates remembered 50 per cent or less of what was read.

Key technique

Bear in mind, in relation to that test, that:

1 They were in a learning scenario which should have conditioned them to concentrate on what was being said and one would have expected an above average result.

2 The questions were posed immediately after the passage was read. One can only imagine the results had there been a gap before asking the questions.

5 *If the communication is interactive* (for example *via* conversation or informal presentation with invited delegate comment, question, etc.) a person should remember of the content   *... about 70%*

6 *If the communication takes place in a learning situation* (for example a trainee talking their way through a process) they should remember of the commentary   *... about 90%*

This is the reasoning behind asking students to talk their way through a particular process, the process of them actually commentating on their actions helps fix the facts in the mind.

The above data is reminiscent of the old saying

What people do they learn
What people see they remember
What people hear they forget

– great news for telephone devotees!

Body language – the added communicator
■ ■ ■

Obviously with situations numbered 1–4 something is lacking since at least half of the content is being forgotten. What

is it that is lacking? The secret lies in what is not said or conveyed as much as what is said or conveyed.

Case study 2.4
THE ORIGINATOR'S RESPONSIBILITY

In the last sentence I did not emphasise the word 'not' – did you have to
re-read it to get the point? If you did, I apologise but it was deliberate to
try to demonstrate that sometimes we see what we think will be on the
page rather than what is there. (This is one of the reasons for many of us
finding it difficult to proof-read our own work.) In that instance, the fault
was mine in not emphasising the word 'not' in order to try to make the
message and the point that much clearer.

Key technique

The golden rule of writing is that if the reader does not understand the
message then it is the writer's fault since (s)he has not expressed
themselves in the clearest way and with the interests of the reader in
mind. We could translate this rule into use in considering telephone
conversation: if the listener does not understand the message it is the
originator's fault not that of the respondent.

The problem of getting our message across by remote
communication (ie the telephone) should not be underestimated. When we are face to face we are able to convey a
great deal by posture, tone and attitude – indeed the whole
range of conscious and sub-conscious body language by
which human beings interface. Our bodies talk for us, often
far more effectively than our tongues ever can. The subconscious language emanating from our bodies is completely
absent when we are linked only by the phone and, despite
our best efforts, we may be working at well under 50 per
cent effectiveness.

Case study 2.5

CAN'T READ YOUR HAND SIGNALS OVER THE PHONE

Not being fluent in French the administrator found it difficult to converse with French-speaking applicants over the phone, most of whom had similar difficulties speaking English, even though they had studied the language. However, when subsequently they met they were bemused to find their comprehension difficulties virtually disappeared. 'I can't understand why we can get by now, when we found it so difficult last week on the phone', said the administrator. 'It's quite simple really – when you are face to face as much as 40–50 per cent of effective communication may be achieved by body language and, particularly with a foreign language, by mime and/or gesture, which is obviously impossible over the phone.'

Key technique

Relying on the phone as a means of real and sole communication is unsatisfactory. Apart from the loss of the additional dimension of understanding granted by body language, human beings generally prefer human contact and a disembodied voice (particularly one we do not know) does not satisfy this preference. When surveyed as to preferences for receiving information and generating communication the order of preference placed a face to face encounter in prime position with telephoned messages almost last.

25

Note:

1 Intriguingly, Desmond Morris recounts in *The Human Animal* (BBC Books) that before they start talking on the phone, the Japanese, who normally bow to each other when they meet, exchange bows even though unable to see each other. Indeed, when presenting the national news on television Japanese newscasters bow to their invisible audience.

2 Devices now exist so that a switchboard dealing with international calls can identify from which country an incoming call has been made so that an operator, able to speak in the language of that country, can

answer the call. Not only does this aid communication and reduce the initial difficulty inherent in such calls, but also it is a valuable public relations exercise.

Determining the use of the telephone
■ ■ ■

If we do not think about what we are doing, our use of the telephone can be automatic. We can be in touch with our target in seconds and able nowadays to hear them as clearly as if they were in the same room. However, the question must be posed – are we really as ready for this instant cerebral connection as our phone is for the instant tele-connection? Just because we can be in touch virtually instantly and can talk to our target within seconds, it does not mean that we are ready to try to achieve communication with them.

26

What are the alternatives?

The somewhat worrying statistics in both Chapter One and above will have demonstrated the need for far greater care in endeavouring to take and make successful calls. We may have been deluding ourselves about our telephone manner rather like the manager who proudly claims that (s)he knows everything that their staff are thinking. This is a classic managerial delusion since even if everyone tells you they are being quite open and honest you can never really know, often until it is too late. There is always some part of our brain that will retain our most private thoughts – perhaps known only to ourselves.

We need to beware the arrogance and complacency of believing as we may have done that all our calls were models of clarity and we were achieving a near perfect performance and it was only the awkward customers with which we had to deal who were the instigators of any difficulties. Further research from America indicates that 94 per cent of the population simply wish to get on with everyone. Initially, in the UK, one can feel quite relieved that this leaves only 6 per cent who can be tough on the phone until you realise that even that proportion applied to a population of 56,000,000 means there can be well over 3,000,000 people who could be difficult to deal with, and that we can turn some of the placid 94 per cent into tough callers if we don't deal with them adequately!

In view of all these bad vibes, we can perhaps be forgiven for instinctively feeling we should never make another phone call other than to the speaking clock or to obtain the latest cricket score or weather forecast. This would be absurd but it is worth examining the alternatives since they may provide some clues as to why such alternatives may be more effective means of communication. The simplest alternative to making a call (or using e-mail) is to send a note or write a letter, not that this is likely to satisfy the modern-day need for instant response.

27

Composing yourself before composing the message
■ ■ ■

In order to write we have to sit down and compose ourselves before we compose our letter. Not least, we need to find a flat surface, paper and a pen. Finding and marshalling these items takes time. Even if we are using technology we need to switch on our typewriter and feed in some paper, or to boot up the word processor and check the printer has paper and so on. These 'delays' are of course compounded by the fact that even using the latest technology we cannot write as fast as we can speak and thus our thought processes are themselves slowed by the output speed. Similarly, other than the best keyboard operators, few of us can type as quickly as we can think. Such 'delays', frustrating as they may be at times, might perhaps be regarded as blessings in disguise, since they provide thinking time and force us to consider the task ahead. They require us to think about what it is we are going to say – we may even have time to consider alternative phrases and to choose one over another. We have time to reconsider whether we use our original draft content, or whether we revise the form and content, alter the message and so on. We may even reconsider our whole strategy for dealing with the matter. The use of a word processor of course aids us in this endeavour. Altering phrases, sentences, whole paragraphs, deleting chunks of text and substituting others is made so easy that we can play around with the message *ad infinitum*. Whatever else it does, it helps us with the process of polishing the item we wish to produce so that it most accurately reflects on paper what we wish to say.

Whatever we do and however we alter our original message, we can be sure of three things:

1 that having the capacity to rewrite, revise and polish our message should result in our final version being 'better' than our first;

2 that whatever we put in the letter is finite; and

3 no-one can interrupt us or interfere with the way we want to display our thoughts on paper.

Obviously the second point above is one reason for preferring the phone on occasion. Whatever we put in writing is permanently there – whatever we say on the phone (tape-recorded conversations apart, see Chapter Thirteen) can actually be denied, which may provide a considerable advantage in avoiding precedents and providing flexibility after the event.

However, nothing could be further from this scenario than our phone call which

1 requires an instant message;

2 entails infinite capacity to vary the message; and

3 requires constant opportunities for interruption causing us to lose our flow, overlook points and be diverted into entirely tangential matters (even, in our view, irrelevant) to our original purpose.

The impulsive act
■ ■ ■

Composing a written message is a definite and deliberate act, it requires commitment, and, for its execution, requires the application of a skill which we were taught in what some may regard as tortuous sessions in the classroom. Whilst any drawing skills we possess may be instinctive, writing skills can only ever be derived from training, coaching and practice. Not only did we need to learn the letters we also had to learn how to shape them. Even if the word processor can now do these things for us, and, with the latest technology, even check our grammar, we still need to develop the thought process that enables us to compose our message (try asking the spell-check to do that!). This self-same deliberation and step-by-step procedure is not present (more accurately, is often entirely lacking) when we come to the spoken word. We don't have to organise ourselves in order to speak, so we can be lulled into a false sense of security and not do so. Our words are there ready to be spoken, ready to be spewed out in an unstructured stream, ready to pour down the telephone and into our respondent's ear virtually before we have thought of them. Indeed in conversation we often fail to finish sentences for a variety of reasons.

- We may sense or suspect from the other person's body language that they know what we mean – or indeed know it and reject it – in which case we may be able to change tack and/or prepare for confrontation.

- We may be interrupted verbally by the other party.

- We interrupt ourselves, which is not the bad sign it may appear, since it demonstrates that we are thinking and rethinking, and even taking into account the attitude of the other party, even as we talk.

Most of us required little or no training in order to learn how to speak, we literally picked it up as we went along and were corrected by parents and teachers. Secure in the knowledge that we now know 'how to do it', we feel equipped to deal with the medium by which our words can hit the ear of our respondent. Thus deluded by superb confidence in our own ability to speak we tend to take an impulsive act – we pick up the phone, our instant access device. In less than ten seconds from giving in to our impulse (a fraction of the time it would have taken us to prepare to write, let alone compose, a letter, even using e-mail) we could be in conversation with our target and there we are: in verbal communication with our target. The trouble is that often we are not – in verbal communication that is. We may be in contact and we may indeed be spewing forth the words, but

- are these really the words we wished to use?

- are they the right words for this person and this situation?

- did we really mean to say that in that way?

- did we really want to use that tone?

The real trouble is that in succumbing to the impulsive act of picking up the phone we may not be at all ready for the dynamic interplay we have now initiated. Unlike receiving a written reply to our letter, which may have taken us some time to compose, and then having in turn some time (which might be as long as weeks but will certainly be minutes) to consider our respondent's response, we are now in the position of needing to respond ourselves to the instant response of our respondent. Instead of the sedate end to end play of a leisurely bowls match, we are involved in the verbal equivalent of a tennis match with the world number one seed. Instead of time to consider our tactics in response to the last wood clipping the jack before we select our next wood, we have to try and reply to the equivalent of a service ace bearing down on us at over 730 mph (ie the speed of sound). In short, in addition to the problems of the device itself, and to communications obstructions, we add to our difficulties simply by not thinking through the effect of the process we have initiated. It is hardly any wonder if we are 'aced' by those who are more prepared than us for the tough call.

Case study 2.6

ORIENTAL TAKE-AWAY

When considering a project in countries in the East, considerable time, far longer than the equivalent in the West, will be taken by those responsible. Indeed, in many instances several people or teams will be asked to consider the same task and to make parallel (or even divergent) recommendations. Whilst such thinking and planning time may be, in our eyes, prolonged, when it comes to execution, the time spent tends to be much shorter and overall the project often consumes less time than it would in the West. In spending time thinking out the problems, alternative solutions present themselves, and can be incorporated into the plan.

31

Key technique

Lack of thinking time may get the job started sooner but ended later, as any initial time advantage tends to be dissipated by the need to sort out problems during execution that should have been foreseen – and planned and catered for – during the planning (thinking) period.

Gaining a breathing space
■ ■ ■

If when we phone we have not given ourselves at least the equivalent time that we would spend in arranging paper, desk and pen before starting a letter and the time we spend in composing our message then we may well find we have given up control over the encounter that we would otherwise have retained. Our target is there with us electronically and can interrupt and alter our thoughts virtually without any consideration. It's as if in adding words to the letter the page started to answer back. Whilst this may be an amusing scenario that could have been lifted from the trial scene in *Alice's Adven-*

tures in Wonderland, it is hardly helpful when all we want to do is complete our message.

Uses and abuses of the phone
■ ■ ■

This is not meant to imply that we should never use the phone, merely that we need to plan for its use, as we do when we start to write a letter, and that if we do then we may actually be both more successful in using it as a communication medium and in avoiding a proportion of the tough calls we may otherwise encounter. The following should not be taken as absolutes but as ideals. We should use, or not use, the phone in the circumstances suggested but we must recognise that reality and circumstance may dictate that regardless of whether it is ideal or not, we may have to use the medium despite all its inherent disadvantages. Under such circumstances we need to be alert to, and ready to compensate for, the inherent drawbacks – perhaps using other communication means to augment what we can achieve over the phone.

Ideal uses

Factual

1 *Information dissemination:* making appointments, resolving misunderstandings over arrangements, confirming bookings and so on. Basically this can be summed up in the words. 'If you can arrange it by phone it is almost certainly going to cost you a fraction of what it would cost if it were dealt with by post or, worse still in cost terms (though not possibly in terms of target rapport), by personal visit and is certainly going to be arranged far more swiftly'.

Case study 2.7
ROBBERY ON THE INFORMATION HIGHWAY

Benchmark Research, on behalf of PhoneLinK (creators of Tel-Me), an on-line business information service, stated in 1995 following a survey that they had conducted, that businessmen and their personal assistants can spend on average up to 10 per cent (ie up to four hours) of their time each week obtaining basic business information – phone numbers, train times and company information, etc.

2 *Data determining:* chasing original information or data supplementary to that already received. As a means of impact to urge the provision of data, a personal telephone call is by far the best substitute for personal presence, it certainly has more power than a memo (which can always be lost accidentally or even deliberately!).

3 *Elucidation and query elimination:* requiring explanation or clarification of something already conveyed to the person making the call.

33

Neutral uses

(Meaning that the phone can be used, but is probably best used for these purposes as secondary, or back up, means.)

Contact-making and updating: keeping in touch. In this instance the phone can only ever be a substitute for meeting but if distances are considerable there may be no alternative.

Speculative uses

Cold calling (see Chapter Ten): generating (or attempting to generate) business by the scattergun approach ie 'If I ring enough people with details of my product/service I am bound to find some who will take me up'.

Contractual uses

1 *Ordering goods or services* (or information about them): The use of the phone for this purpose is probably its greatest growth potential. An American survey disclosed that as many people who disliked going to the dentist, disliked going to the supermarket for their basic shopping. This has been used to support the concept of 'teleselling' ie buying *via* a telephone link to a visual display of products using a television, which, somewhat reasonably it is argued, would appeal to such consumers. In the UK Anderson Consulting has opened Smart Store Europe in Windsor, Berkshire, to demonstrate the computer systems available for such 'shopping by screen'.

2 *Advising re non-delivery of goods* etc, or delivery of faulty or sub-standard goods or services, or any instance where dissatisfaction has occurred (but see Abuses below).

34

Discussion

With matters of mutual interest where the parties know each other and know the subject matter (but not otherwise).

Abuses

1 *Conducting a meeting:* Although video-conferencing can be very effective, particularly where the members are geographically separated so that there may be no other realistic alternative, using the traditional phone for this purpose can limit the effectiveness of any meeting of any length. Particularly since much of the communication during a meeting is conducted by the body language of the members which is impossible over the phone.*

2 *Discussing terms or any matter which is involved or likely to be disputed.* Although it is possible to conduct such business successfully on the phone it is fraught with difficulty

* See *Manipulating Meetings*, Martin, Pitman Publishing, 1994.

and requires very careful planning and execution. It really should only be attempted if a physical meeting is out of the question and/or the basis of the argument has already been put in writing and sent to the other party so that before the call some consensus – at least about the subject – already exists.

3 *Lodging a complaint where there may be a dispute concerning the facts.* Once again there may be no alternative, but the phone should be used only as the second stage – the case should have already been put in writing in an attempt to establish the facts.

4 *Giving directions or instructions which are anything other than very straightforward or simple.* Once again, written guidance sent in advance – particularly by fax if time is short – may be preferable since at least then both parties have something tangible to consider.

35

5 *Speculative phone calls without warning.* These do not necessarily relate to selling but nevertheless can interrupt the recipient and cause irritation which will mitigate against calm consideration of the subject matter. It may be preferable (ie more successful although possibly not as cost-effective) to canvas by post first offering a freephone number for interested parties to call back.

3

Those who live by the phone . . .

Key learning points

1 Identifying and learning to avoid five false assumptions related to telephoning should help minimise the chance of taking and losing tough calls.

2 We need to have in our mind at all times that by far the best way of dealing with tough calls is to avoid their incidence – that is to ensure that we don't create them in the first place. By improving our approach and our systems the risk of creating tough calls should be minimised.

3 We need to realise that everyone will not see things in the same way as we do and consider how to achieve our desired result accordingly. Our ultimate goal should always be in the forefront of our mind.

4 Setting out to anticipate tough calls and considering ways in which we can handle them should enable us to avoid the worst calls.

Building on foundations
■ ■ ■

What we have examined so far are the misconceptions on which many calls are based. We have identified the barriers that will impede the reception and acceptance of our calls, and considered the difficulties of achieving true communication through the telephone – a remote contact medium. The fact that this is a two way process must always be considered:

- what we expect we should be prepared to give;

- what mannerisms and tactics we dislike we should avoid using;

- what deceptions we mistrust and abhor we should not use, and so on.

The five false assumptions
■ ■ ■

In developing a telephone manner capable of dealing with toughness, we need first to rid ourselves of misconceptions including (not necessarily exclusively) the following five false assumptions. All too often we are trapped into making assumptions even though research indicates that over 85 per cent of assumptions made are actually false.

Assumption 1 – The 'power cocoon'

If we have reached a position of some authority in our organisation we may have become so used to the deference and prestige that such a position grants us that we find it increasingly difficult to appreciate, still less agree with, the viewpoints of others. In some organisations it is not just senior managers but virtually the whole organisation that becomes so cocooned. (This is a danger outside and beyond the scope of this book since it can lead to an arrogance that is potentially very dangerous. The recession humbled and put out of business a number of organisations who thought that they knew it all and did not need to heed the 'other person's' point of view.)

The underlying belief of the cocooned is that their factory, office, unit or whatever is actually the centre of the world to which virtually everything else is subordinate. It can come as a cruel shock when it is realised that not everyone outside the cocoon thinks or acts as we do, or as we think they should. The thought of there being another viewpoint or of people not being prepared to do things in the way that we want them done is impossible to contemplate. If this is a dangerous delusion within the confines of our own society, consider how much more difficult it becomes when trying to interface with those from different countries, ethnic origins and cultures from our own. With such callers we will not even have the same outlook.

39

Case study 3.1

MEDICAL DISORDERLY

The American matron was obviously someone used to authority and to instant obedience. Whilst this may have cut considerable ice within her own organisation it failed to do so externally. She required some casual domestic assistance in her home and rang an agency late one Friday afternoon. *'Of course we can help,'* replied the assistant *'I'll send you our registration pack and as soon as we receive your registration form, we'll start a search for someone to suit your requirements. I must warn you, however, that it is likely to take a few weeks – and longer if you have any specific or unusual requirements.'*

'I've no time for all that, I can just dictate the details to you over the phone now, I need someone immediately you see.'

'Well, we're not supposed to work that way but if you like I'll fax you the forms to fill in. If you give me the details over the phone, whilst you are completing the forms and sending them back we can be looking for you – that should help cut down the delay a little.'

'No. I want you to fill in the forms for me, I want someone straight away.'

'Well we're not supposed to work that way. I'll fill in as much as I can before I fax the items to you but you must complete the personal details and sign the registration form and return it.'

'I'll fax it back to you straightaway.'

'No, I am sorry but it must be sent in the reply paid envelope, or handed back to us so that we have an original signed registration form. If you put it in the post as soon as you've completed it we should receive it first thing on Monday.'

Over the weekend the matron phoned the agency four times leaving increasingly strident messages stressing the urgency of her situation and the fact that she wanted action. The director of the agency telephoned her on Monday.

'Hallo Ms Holden, I have just been listening to our answerphone and was a little surprised to find four messages from you.'

'Yes I am very annoyed that I had to phone four times – don't you clear your messages?'

'Of course but our office is only open from Monday to Friday – as stated in the information pack we faxed to you on Friday evening.'

'Oh, I haven't had time to read that. Now where's this domestic? I need her immediately.'

'I'm awfully sorry but as you were told when you rang and as it points out in the information pack it does tend to take at least two to three weeks to find someone suitable.'

'That's no good to me – I want someone to start straightaway.'

'I appreciate the urgency but I must point out that even if we had someone suitable we could not send them to you as you have not returned the registration form we partially completed for you.'

'I can't be bothered to fill all that in.'

'Then I am sorry but we cannot make any progress until you do.'

'I . . . I . . . I've never been spoken to like this before.'

40

Key techniques

1 Being used to saying 'do this' and it being done can lead to a sense of absolute power. It can come as a shock when dealing with an outsider, to whom such internal power means nothing, to realise that power is only applicable within its source.

2   The matron had not realised that her desired result – the placing of a domestic assistant – was more likely to be achieved by treating the outsider as an equal rather than as one of her underlings (not accepting that such an attitude is the best way to treat any underling in any event). She felt that force was the only way to achieve what she wanted, overlooking the fact that, particularly in the UK, very often our temperament rebels against such an attitude.

3   It is unlikely that she would be able to give medical care to a patient without obtaining information about them – why should she feel that the agency could act without information concerning her exact requirements?

4   From the agency angle, tact was used to try to defuse a potentially intemperate call. They were prepared to bend their rules (three times) in order to help, but not to break them.

5   Americans, as well as many continentals, seem to us in the UK (where we have traditionally tended to be far more diffident) to be very assertive. There may be nothing wrong with this (although in this instance the attitude was akin to aggression) we simply need to recognise this so that we can deal with such culture differences. As business and telephone networks become more 'globalised' we may expect more calls from those who do not see things in the same way as we do.

6   Whilst respect may be expected, compliance with one's own viewpoint cannot simply be commanded, it needs to be sought.

41

If the power cocoon creates a false impression of all-embracing power it should not be overlooked that it may also lull us into a false sense of security in our ability to gain our ultimate objective even though we have created (and ought to be aware that we have created) an instant antipathy. This is virtually certain to create a tough business call which will normally rebound to our loss. Using force unfairly does tend to backfire and to work against our best interests. Using the power we possess may massage our ego but may also ensure that we defeat our own aim.

Case study 3.2

HOW NOT TO WIN FRIENDS . . .

At short notice the agency had arranged to supply a client with a temporary employee on a specified date, which the client then tried to bring forward. On learning that the employee was not available until the date of their original request, the client decided to withdraw her offer. In taking this decision she became liable to pay a small administration charge which was deducted from the fee she had paid. The balance was sent to her. Her husband, a director of his own company, telephoned the agency:

'As you've been unable to supply this temp. I want the whole of our fee back but you've only sent part of it.'

'As explained to your wife, we have returned your fee, less our normal administration charge.'

'That's not good enough, your service is appalling, you've been unable to supply this person, you've taken our money under false pretences and I want it all back.'

'I'm sorry, I really cannot accept any of what you are saying. I see from the file in front of me that we have your wife's written acceptance of our terms, and that having given us a statement of her requirements when she registered, subsequently she changed those requirements. The young lady cannot start until the original date – two weeks after the date your wife now specifies – which is of course a date which she changed. We offered to find someone else in the time available but your wife said this was not acceptable and opted for the return of her fee.'

'I think that's a disgraceful way to run a business. You've supplied poor quality staff in the past and now you're charging us for doing nothing.'

'I don't think that is the case at all. Looking through the file I see that your wife indicated on each occasion we have supplied her with someone that they were satisfactory. This time we carried out a great deal of work and additionally tried to help at short notice and to satisfy changes indicated by your wife. We were still prepared to find an alternative but this was not acceptable to her.'

'Hmmm, well I'll tell you what – let's start again – can you take the refund back and try and find us an alternative employee?'

'No, bearing in mind the comments you have just made, I'm not prepared to do that.'

Key technique

The ultimate desired result sought by the client's husband was a favour from the agency if he could not force a full refund. Acting strictly in accordance with its terms, to which his wife had previously signed her agreement, the agency held all the cards in this tough call. It had its records showing the previous satisfied history of the relationship and could indicate it was acting completely fairly. By exaggerating and lying to try to gain a negotiating edge, the client placed himself in an untenable position when subsequently trying to obtain a 'favour'. The advantage of having paperwork available when taking (or making) a tough call cannot be emphasised too strongly. There is an inherent strength (which is almost certainly reflected in the tone used and thus in the confidence available when arguing the case) which can be drawn from relying on data or records immediately available and, as a result, exaggeration and lying can backfire. Not for nothing have records been called the lifeblood of the organisation.

43

Note: The agency could have pointed out that as the booking and the request had all been made in the caller's wife's name, their contract was with her and they had no need to discuss matters with him at all. It is pointless to make such a point unless things become really difficult as it is likely to achieve little other than further irritation. Nevertheless a realisation of the exact relationship of the caller can be very valuable – ignorance of the terms of a contract is dangerous – see Case Study 4.4).

Assumption 2 – My priority is your priority

This assumption echoes the attitude evinced by the matron in Case Study 3.1. Simply because we have a burning number one priority does not mean that our respondent will have the same priority, especially if our request comes to them out of the blue, and even more so when the reason behind the urgency is inefficiency or lack of planning on the part of the person making the call. Indeed, here the effect may be the very opposite of what we want unless we handle the situation very carefully.

Case study 3.3

YOU SHOULD HAVE THOUGHT OF THAT

Having completed the delayed proof-reading of a book for a publisher (not this book or this publisher!) I turned to other work, delayed because the proofs themselves had been poorly presented and badly delayed. Then the fax clattered out a message from the publisher asking for comments on some proposed publicity documentation. I rang the contact.

'Look I've got these four pages – when do you want my comments?'

'Tomorrow.'

'I'm sorry but that's impossible, I'm out all day tomorrow and in fact I'm leaving in a few minutes for a meeting which I've delayed because of dealing with work caused by the problems with your proofs. I can't put that meeting off again.'

'But I have to go to press tomorrow.

'Well I'm sorry but you'll have to do it without my input – I am working on matters which I delayed because you delayed the proofs – my other work must have some priority now.'

Key techniques

1 The fax is a marvellous device. Unfortunately it is also a marvellous accessory – both before and after the act - to insufficient planning. In this case there was no reason why the publicity material could not have been generated weeks beforehand giving more than sufficient time for consideration. Such lack of planning or inefficiency, or simply a failure to appreciate that other people have other priorities, may lead us directly into tough or unsuccessful calls.

2 The rudeness of simply faxing documentation which requires a considerable amount of work on the part of the recipient without

   a ringing them first to ask if they can help within a tight time-frame, and

   b checking if the recipient is actually there and

   c checking that they could do as asked (particularly when time is short), can generate a negative reaction in many people. Far better to ring and say 'Terribly sorry, we've got a real emergency here, we overlooked the need to generate publicity material and now we need it very urgently. Could I possibly fax it to you so you could look at it straightaway?' Persuasion tends to be better than force.

Notes:

1 The 'softly softly catchee monkee' approach may work the first time and possibly the second, but it is unlikely to be effective if it is used repeatedly to cover constant inefficiency. This really can rebound against the caller.

2 Real aggravation resulted on another occasion when an adviser dropped everything, worked through a lunch break to generate what was required and rang back only to find that the person who had requested the urgent work was taking an extended lunch hour to do some shopping! What a nice warm feeling that gave the adviser, and how prepared she was to help next time! Such action simply stores up the possibility of a tough (failed) call next time and yet could have been easily avoided by making another call such as *'Terribly sorry to have landed that rush job on you like that, I do appreciate your input, I've got to rush off to another meeting now and I won't be back until [time] so, if it's OK, I'll ring you then to see how you are getting on.'*

It may be a pack of lies but it's a device which stops the other party ringing back and finding out that the important business 'meeting' was actually personal 'shopping', probably carries them along to do the job, and may help attain the timescale within which you are working. Three advantages plus the overwhelming positive effect that a further tough call has probably been avoided.

Warning: This 'I'll ring you back at [time]' comment is a classic piece of manipulation. Instead of questioning the basis of the call, the respondent's attention is focused on the need to be available at the time suggested. This verbal *legerdemain* is an effective ploy unless the respondent is concentrating on the reason for the call. If not, they may find themselves agreeing to a further commitment – to take that call.

45

Setting the ground rules

This could also be entitled 'Getting the specification agreed'. It may be helpful, although it needs to be done tactfully and cannot be broached to all-comers, with those with whom we are in regular contact to set some ground rules. In the instance related in Case Study 3.3, I was so annoyed by the calm assumptions that I was both there and free and also could drop everything to deal with an urgent problem not of my making that I drew up some ground rules for future dealings. An example is set out below.

Setting guidelines

1 Provided a timetable had been agreed a deadline would always be met.

2 In the unlikely event that making the deadline was impossible adequate notice would be given.

3 In emergencies obviously help would be provided.

4 Before faxing, a check should be made to ensure someone was there to receive the message not to assume that this was the case (obviously this point is less important with larger organisations – although regardless of size, if the answer lies with, or action is required by, one individual and (s)he is away, on holiday, dead or whatever, the fact that someone else actually receives the fax is of no help).

5 Reasonable time for input and reply should be allowed.

Taking such action, that is setting out what is and is not expected makes it clear where the responsibilities of each party lie – tough call avoided – no tempers raised – everyone happy – problem sorted!

Assumption 3 – I have the time now so you must have too

Much of the problem with tough business calls revolves round their timing and the apparent total lack of realisation by those that make them that simply because now is a good time for them to ring you that it may not at all be a good time for the respondent to talk to the caller.

Hint: Stop the caller in their tracks and state that it is inconvenient and that you will ring them back later in the day – but do make sure you do so.

Case study 3.4

WHAT AN IMPRESSION

The director was interviewing an applicant for the position of manager of one of the departments in his organisation. A few minutes into the interview the phone rang and the director spent a minute or so chatting to the caller. After a few more minutes the phone rang again and again minutes were consumed on the call. Ten minutes later the phone rang again and the director became engaged in a heated discussion for several minutes. During this call the applicant scribbled some words on a piece of paper, placed it in front of the director and walked out. The note read *'Dear Mr Jones, Since, obviously, my interview is of so much less importance than your phone calls, I'll leave you to them. I have no wish to work for an organisation so lacking in basic courtesy.'*

47

Key techniques

1   In such a situation the phone should have been taken off the hook or calls could simply have been diverted. If neither was possible, a simple *'Sorry I can't speak to you at the moment, I'm in an interview, I'll ring you back in an hour,'* should satisfy the impatient callers as well as the patient listener.

2   When a colleague of mine makes a call, he always asks if it is convenient to discuss matters. Such calls can, because they tend to relate to quite technical and legal subjects, require considerable time investment. Because of such politeness, even if it is extremely inconvenient, few respondents ever put him off and so he gets his own way – a discussion of his business at his time of calling.

Notes:

1   Of course it should not be overlooked that if you do take the call at least it means the other party is paying for it –

ringing back will cost you. Of course when you do call back it may then be inconvenient to the other party in turn, so it may be wise to fix a mutually convenient time. The advantage of the 'ring back' is that both parties have time to prepare, which may, despite the delay, result in a more effective call.

2 When selling programmes for a charity carnival, a young colleague always turned in far better figures than everyone else. One night I happened to hear his *spiel*: *'I am sorry to bother you but we wondered whether you would be able to help a handicapped child by spending a few pence to buy a souvenir programme'*. Far more effective than *'We're selling programmes for our carnival – they cost 25p each – how many would you like?'* They say that 'manners maketh the man' – they may also help attain successful (ie non-tough) calls.

48

Assumption 4 – The other party will agree with our assessment that decision time is now

This can also be defined as the 'fools rush in' technique. Some people feel that if they create a sense of urgency they can push the respondent into a decision. This is beloved of cold calling salesmen and saleswomen and obviously it works on some poor innocents. The concept is that if you agree now then you can gain an advantageous price. Whilst fine in itself often there is a hidden agenda and the 'rush, rush, rush' tempo may actually be counterproductive.

Case study 3.5
DOUBLE DEALING

'Hi there Mr Jones, it's George from Ben Nevis Double Glazing – you remember I left you the quote for the replacement of your rear windows.'

'Oh yes, thanks.' (What Mr Jones really thinks is *'Oh hell, it's that pain again – I only agreed to look at the quote to get him off my doorstep.'*)

'I just wanted to tell you that time is running out and the company has just told me of a price increase that they are putting in that will affect all orders placed after tomorrow.'

'But I want to think about this for a few days.' (Mr Jones is really thinking *'How do I get out of this? It's far too expensive for me.'*)

'Yes, I'm sure but that thinking time could cost you quite a lot of money. How about if I pop round now and explain the extra costs and collect your order . . .'

Key techniques

1 In the same way that he isn't saying what he is thinking, unless he is a complete innocent, Mr Jones probably realises (correctly) that neither is the salesman saying what he is thinking. What may be the background to the call is that the salesman's commission looks pretty poor this month and he is trying to bolster it by producing a sale.

2 It might be more effective for the salesman to tell the truth and actually say that that is why he wants the order. At least this could play on Mr Jones' sympathy, although trying for the sympathy vote is not a very reliable or successful card to play. Indeed, the salesman might make the deal more attractive by offering to share some of his commission with Mr Jones which just might make it less expensive so that it becomes more tempting to Mr Jones.

3 By offering to 'pop round' the salesman actually grants control to the client who can say 'no' for a variety of reasons. It might be more effective not to bother with the phone at all which poses difficulties in closing a sale, but simply to turn up at the house.

49

Assumption 5 – The other party has a similar depth of understanding and appreciation of the matter to our own and can agree with our assessment of the way forward

What is attempted here is to bulldoze an agreement from the other party because, quite obviously, there really isn't any alternative. We are actually making two assumptions here:

1 the 'TINA' concept – There Is No Alternative – which may have been correct when used in another context by Margaret Thatcher but is unlikely to be so in other instances; and

2 the other party will agree with the need for a decision.

If the person we are calling lacks our perception of the problem or the matter under discussion then it may become very difficult to gain any rapport. We may indeed finish – as we started – on two separate planes. In addition, there is an insult inherent in such a call – that regardless of any input from the respondent the decision will remain the same.

Case study 3.6

NO LONGER NEEDED

'Oh Mrs Saville, I'm glad I caught you. We've been looking at these figures you've put together and have come to a conclusion.'

'A conclusion? – But there are a number of alternatives and a few more I've thought of since I put that report together. I thought you asked me to work up a discussion document?'

'Yes, I know but there is really only one which really works . . . and we agree that we should make you redundant from Friday week.'

'But I was indicating that it might be better to slim the hours of several people so that you could still maintain a complete service rather than losing a whole person.'

'No, we don't think that will work. Now about the arrangements for you leaving us . . .'

Key technique

To anyone conscious of the importance of personal relationships it seems impossible that such a conversation could take place over a phone, but it did and that real-life example is by no means unique. Using the phone for such a purpose is totally incorrect since it can only create aggravation and in such an instance almost certainly land the employer in an industrial tribunal and losing the action.

Assuming again

Any assumption of agreement with our own assessment, views or version of events, is virtually guaranteed to start a tough call – or more likely a number of calls that could become tougher and tougher.

51

4

. . .

Getting and improving the phoning habit

Key learning points

1 An increasing proportion of the population has access to a phone and is prepared to use it to try to obtain instant solutions to their problems.

2 Increased use of the medium leads to increased confidence in using it and we must be prepared for this development.

3 Society generally is becoming more assertive (even aggressive) and we need to be prepared to deal with such demanding behaviour and requirements.

4 Listening to ourselves on the phone and developing a checklist to train ourselves to handle our calls more effectively may help us achieve greater success in handling tough calls.

Telephiles and telephobes

■ ■ ■

The Henley Forecasting Group carried out a study in 1994 and discovered that nearly 50 per cent of the UK population are prepared to use the phone and are confident in their use of it to carry on business. They described these consumers as 'telephiles'. Conversely only 16 per cent are 'telephobes' – people who use the phone as little as possible. The remainder of the population don't necessarily enjoy using the phone but are prepared to do so. Thus a substantial proportion of the population is becoming increasingly proficient in and confident about their use of the phone. Indeed one has only to listen to the radio to realise how used people are becoming to the phone as a communication medium. There seem to be an ever-increasing number of programmes which encourage (indeed depend for their existence) on listeners phoning in to put forward their points of view. Whilst a number of such callers obviously find difficulty expressing their thoughts clearly (and some may not have heard what was said very accurately – see Case Study 2.2), nevertheless most are able to put over their points and add to the debate. As part of the research on communication during seminars referred to earlier, I asked the same delegates to indicate who liked dealing with difficult or awkward matters over the telephone. Only 20 (out of around 150) stated that they did and, when questioned, all of them confirmed that their approach was to prepare carefully for the encounter before placing the call. In most cases this involved making detailed notes of all aspects of the subject.

The Henley research reflects the trend in our society towards increased outspokenness, assertiveness and even aggression. Whilst this may be welcomed from some viewpoints we need to realise that here we have a recipe which can result in the creation of an increasing number of tough calls, particularly if the initial response is either receipt of the call by someone like 'bored voice' in Case Study 6.3 or irritating delay whilst listening to what were obviously totally insincere apologies such as those in Case Study 5.2, or a casual dismissal of contractual terms – or an uninspiring selection of music – or possibly a combination of any of the four!

Aggravation
■ ■ ■

The fact that our society is becoming far more assertive – even to the point of aggression – may be the result of the severe recession of the late 1980s and early 1990s. Although this latest recession was no more severe than that of the 1930s (indeed in many ways that in the 1930s was more severe), the one essential difference was that those who lost, (and in some cases lost everything), had started off with far more than their grandparents had in the 1930s. When you do not have much there is little to lose, when you have a great deal and it is lost – the degree of loss is obviously far more severe and the reaction far more hostile.

55

However, no one factor is the cause of this increased assertiveness. Indeed, another cause may be the result of the population being able to see confrontational politics represented by the unedifying spectacle of the Prime Minister and Leader of the Opposition insulting each other twice each week. If such so-called 'leaders' act in such a fashion it is hardly surprising if they are emulated elsewhere.

Case study 4.1

POLITICS – THE ART OF THE IMPOSSIBLE

The confrontational aspect of British politics, particularly Prime Minister's Question Time creates considerable interest. Indeed, in the USA, according to a report in the *Financial Times* of July 1995, it is treated as '15 minutes of knockabout political theatre' which can hardly provide one with the appropriate impression of the respect one would expect to be accorded to the Prime Minister of the United Kingdom. However, this confrontational style, where the most important aspect seems to be to score debating points off one's opponent rather than actually being seen to deal with the serious and pressing problems of the day, is screened constantly and seen to be an example of the behaviour of senior politicians. It is hardly any wonder if society itself then becomes more confrontational in turn. In fact, Parliament is considering changes to the system so that 'a more serious approach' can be taken to Prime Minister's Question Time. The system where one party proposes and another automatically has to oppose whatever is suggested is wasteful enough without showing the two leaders behaving like teenagers in a school debating society.

The assertiveness bordering on aggression may also be derived from seeing so many instances on television in other works of fiction (although Prime Minister's Question Time at Westminster is not seen by many as the fiction it is) where the plot can only be made more interesting if there is conflict and disagreement. If we grow used to seeing actors with whom we can identify in assertive and aggressive situations, we would hardly be human if we did not copy at least some of their characteristics and even their dialogue. Whatever the cause, the result is that assertiveness and aggression now seem to be more the rule than the exception.

We even see this on our roads where the phenomenon of 'road rage' is beginning to cause increasing concern. Otherwise mild mannered men and women, when frustrated by traffic snarl ups and not being able to 'get a move on', or by intentional (and sometimes even unintentional) poor driving or bad manners on the part of another, become transformed into aggressive and dangerous thugs wielding not just their fists but also anything that comes to hand, even including iron bars. Again, the example for such drivers of seeing world class racing drivers indulge in similar behaviour on the race track is hardly helpful.

If as drivers we can understand how road problems can have this effect on otherwise normal human beings (even if we cannot condone or understand them then resorting to violence) we should be able to understand why some of our telephone callers resort to an aggressive manner when we frustrate them by poor service, indifference and inadequate answering systems.

Manners maketh the man – and help avoid the tough call

■ ■ ■

Side by side with this slide into assertive and aggressive ways, has been an apparent lapse from the adoption of good manners. Perhaps this is one of the main reasons for the increase in the incidence of tricky calls. No matter how much we are advised that being calm and arguing in a low key way can improve our chances of success, it is a fact that it is possible to get one's own way by ignoring the niceties of manners, by failing to respect the viewpoint of others and by forcing the sublimation of all other viewpoints but one's own (the attitude evinced in Case Studies 3.1 and 3.2). It may work (although it failed in both those instances) once or even twice, but often those who have lost out previously will find, perhaps next time around, that they have the whip hand and are unlikely to allow the leeway we now seek. Although the American research referred to earlier showed that 94 per cent of people are quite content to 'get by' and 'get along with' others, that still leaves 6 per cent who can be really awkward customers or callers.

57

Our use of the phone is set to increase, a fact which is entirely logical and is predicated by all observers. This is hardly surprising bearing in mind that in America (whose customs do tend to spread across the Atlantic to the UK, whether the countries are separated by a common language or not) they use the phone around four times as much as we do in the UK. With an expected development like this we need to develop adequate defences, manners and habits. One of the best defences is to learn patience, as Benjamin Franklin said 'the man who has patience has everything'. If we have the patience to hear out the grumbler and the assertive caller then we may be able to defuse many of our tough calls.

Listen to me
■ ■ ■

No, not to me but to yourself. When you make or take a call which was tough consider how it went – what were the good points and the bad. Can we re-use the one and avoid the other in the future? This can be difficult as the last thing we should do is to spend so much time listening to our own end of the conversation that we fail to concentrate sufficiently on dealing with the subject in hand. In such a case we could actually create a tough call whilst trying to practise avoiding its incidence!

Of course, simply connecting a tape recorder to the phone is the simplest way of providing a record of the call for later consideration and dissection. Indeed, a number of organisations tape record (particularly) customer calls so that they have a record of what transpired and can use it to improve their service and/or as evidence of what was actually said and promised. This is then available and can be referred to and quoted from in the event of later dispute (although the legality of this may need to be checked).

If deciding against moving to this level of record, brief notes of good and bad points, tactics and arguments can provide a helpful guide the next time around. It should not be overlooked that if there has been a particularly tough and confrontational call, making notes of what transpired at the time may be a valuable defence mechanism should the call be repeated. Being able to state *'I see from the notes that I made at the time that you said . . .'* carries a great deal more weight than *'I thought you said last time . . .'*. Notes taken in this way become evidence and as such tend to carry more weight than memory, particularly bearing in mind the research that suggests that we only retain about 11 per cent of what we hear on the phone anyway. What kind of evidence is that on which to base any further stage in the saga? This of course was the point made in dealing with the call outlined in Case Study 3.2. The file was available to help and after the call was concluded, a resumé of what had transpired during the call was added to it. In this way self-perpetuating evidence is available at all times – to the discomfort of callers who often have only their memory on which to depend – and the research demonstrates how unreliable that can be.

Making and taking

■ ■ ■

Having delineated the scope for the telephone and the advantages and disadvantages of its use we need to pay more attention to its user, bearing in mind the vital point already made that the user can be both instigator of a tough call as well as its respondent. We can be – indeed we often are – in the position of being both prosecuting and defending counsel, situations in which we may find ourselves with consecutive calls. We may be forced to exchange our poacher's coat for that of the gamekeeper very swiftly. With that dual aspect of the matter in mind we need to realise that we may need to develop some tricky footwork (innovative thought, more accurately) to be able to deal effectively with both, although, the tips we can pick up (assertive, 'prosecuting', poaching) for use in a call going in one direction may have immediate application (evasive, 'defending', gamekeeping) in a call coming in the opposite direction. However, in order to deal with both aspects we should consider preparing for the encounter in the same way that barristers do. They prepare for every eventuality and have a rule that they should never ask a question (of a witness) unless they already know the answer, the point being that the unexpected answer may actually damage their case. We need to place ourselves in a similar position which requires comparable, adequate and comprehensive preparation.

59

Case study 4.2

UNSUITABLE

The customer had placed an order for a three piece suite but stipulated that he did not want the one on show which had a stitching flaw and bore a sale label. He was promised a suite 'ex works'. However, when it was delivered he found the flaw and rang the showroom.

'You have delivered this suite.'

'That's right sir, in accordance with your order.'

'Yes, my order, if you have it there you will see that I ordered a suite 'ex works' and stipulated that I did not want the suite on display as there was a flaw in the stitching, and this was written on the order.'

'That's right sir, so we had one delivered from the factory.'

'But it's got the same flaw – you have delivered the suite from your showroom.'

'Oh that's impossible sir – it's been delivered direct from the factory.'

'In that case how do you explain that your branch sale sign is stapled to the underside of the settee?'

Key technique

Asserting what cannot be (i.e. lying) can only lead to tougher calls. Here it led to the store having to reduce the price of the suite below the sale price to avoid having to collect it and replace it with one from the factory as stipulated.

Checking our progress

■ ■ ■

Checking how we conduct ourselves does not need to be done in a vacuum. Since most of us make and take calls each working day it should not take long to jot down what went right (and perhaps more importantly, in terms of making sure we don't do it again, what went wrong) with each call. Thus, the shop assistant in Case Study 4.2 could make a note not to assert things without full knowledge, but rather to check statements first or else make less definite statements 'I don't understand, I think I had better check' would have avoided his subsequent annihilation.

Composing from experience a do-it-yourself checklist can be a sound foundation for training ourselves into a telephone manner that avoids, deals with, or at least defuses the worst of the tough encounters. Since this may take some time it may be helpful to start with a little pump priming in the form of a draft checklist. The checklist below provides an outline guide to the questions we should ask ourselves before we make each call. This checklist is not meant in any way to be exhaustive and readers are encouraged to add their own questions (and to delete any that they feel are inappropriate) so that the list becomes customised to meet their own individual requirements. Obviously not all questions need to be examined in all instances but at least if we have asked ourselves such questions then we will know what we can ignore as well as what we need to consider.

Draft tough call checklist

1 Subject

a Who am I calling?

b What is (s)he like?

c How do they like to be treated?

61

Case study 4.3

CRUDE BY LANGUAGE AND CRUDE IN APPROACH

The director had made it to the top of her organisation but had retained along the way a predilection for crude language which, whilst some found it fascinating, was off-putting to others. She phoned the director of a customer company and in the course of the conversation used some crude language. Her customer felt that he was no longer prepared to put up with this treatment and when it came to arguing about the product price quite deliberately refused to meet the 'last offer' price referred to by the supplier.

*'Do you mean you are not prepared to order any ****ing widgets at all?'*

'No, we are not.'

*'Well you're a bit of a b*****d aren't you!'*

'Basically I am not prepared to buy at that price and not prepared to be subjected to this language either,' said the customer, who then put the phone down and refused to take further calls from the source.

Key technique

The prejudices and preferences of respondents cannot be taken for granted – we need to tread warily. There may be more hanging on a tough call than just conversation.

d Can I use their first name to try to make it more friendly?

Note: It may be helpful to try to avoid the use of the description 'Christian' for a person's first name since nowadays people have a wide variety of religions, most of which are non-Christian. In a 1995 survey across 7,000 people in the UK, USA, India, Japan and Australia, Sponsorship Research International discovered that symbols for the Olympic Movement, McDonald's restaurants, Shell Petrol and Mercedes cars were recognised ahead of the symbol for Christianity, the cross. 'Forename' is more acceptable as well as being strictly accurate in most countries. Further, in some countries, what we in the West refer to as a person's forename, is actually their inhabitant's second name – such customs need to be known and understood to aid rapport and communication.

e Do I know anything about their personal life which I can use to aid rapport?

Case study 4.4

DATA HELPS RAPPORT

The director, concerned at the depression of an adviser, discovered from the adviser's secretary that his wife was seriously ill. Thereafter, at some time during every phone-call he made sure that he asked after her health which gradually built a rapport and mutual understanding which was very valuable since the director wanted support in negotiations with a third party with whom he knew the adviser was very friendly and had influence.

Key techniques

1 Secretaries can be extremely valuable sources of information although enquiry needs to be made tactfully and, under such circumstances, with (at least apparent) genuine concern.

2 Great care needs to be taken with this tactic as one could be seen to be nosy or meddling.

2 *Relationship*

a What is the history of the relationship?

b Have there been problems before?

c What information would it be useful to have available?

d If the person is unknown to me, what can we find out about them, their organisation, products, etc?

e If they are unknown is there any way I can form a link with them (mutual interest, acquaintance, etc,) or use a third party as an introduction?

3 *Timing*

a Is this a good time to make this call? Phoning early on a Monday, or the day after a Bank Holiday, or on the first day a respondent is back from holiday, to do otherwise than simply say 'hello and welcome back' is probably unwise. A better response may be obtained after lunch on that day or on the following day. Immediately stating that one hadn't phoned the previous day 'because I knew you'd be pretty snowed under' might also create a better rapport than otherwise.

b Has the respondent just returned from holiday and will (s)he be harassed and unlikely to wish to discuss the matter, particularly if it is complex or lengthy? If the other party is known and the item is lengthy and/or complex it may be preferable to write or fax a resumé first so that the recipient does not have to come at the matter cold, and to try to improve their retention of the data.

63

  c If I catch this person just as they are going home am I likely to get a quick and favourable decision, or are they likely to resent the intrusion into their relaxation time?

d Would it be better to wait to make this call until they have received [specify] which shows us/me in a good light and they are thus likely to be more receptive to my ideas?

e If I make this call now am I likely to time it so that it pressurises a quick decision or will it aggravate them as they might suspect that is the reason I have so timed it?

4 Purpose

a What is the purpose of this call – what's it for?

b What do I want to achieve from this call?

c Is the person likely to give me what I want to achieve?

d If so, do I need to tread carefully?

- will they want something in return?

- if so, do I want to give this? and

- if not how do I get out of that?

e If not, is there something I can offer which might change their outlook?

f What do I want to gain?

g Do I have anything to offer to attain the gain?

5 Recourse

a Do I need information/a favour from this person?

b If so, what is it (list what is required)?

c Would it be better to ask for the information in advance so I can prepare for the call with the information?

d Is there information from our side which it would be helpful to give to them prior to the call to try and gain agreement and/or understanding?

e Is there any *quid pro quo* I can offer that will balance the favour being asked?

6 Dispute

a Am I ringing since we have a dispute argument?

b If so, what are the facts?

c Are we in the wrong (check the facts and the terms)?

Case study 4.5

GETTING THE TERMS RIGHT

Having advertised regularly in a magazine for some years, the agency was advised that the owners of the magazine had changed. Subsequently, during the UK recession, the agency decided to suspend advertising for two issues and wrote to confirm this.

65

They received the following telephone call:

'Since you are cancelling your advertisement, I must advise you that there will be a cancellation charge and in addition, you will be required to repay your series discount.' [1]

'But we have never agreed any terms with your company.'

'Yes you have, the terms state that late cancellation leads to a 25 per cent charge and cancellation of a series leads to repayment of the series discount.'

'I am sorry but I must disagree – you are referring to the terms issued by your predecessors. No terms have been issued by your company.'

'For the pittance of commission I am paid I am not going to provide new terms for the one instance where an absence of goodwill leads to this kind of problem.' [2]

'That is completely irrelevant. Normally this would be a question of contractual commitments, but in this case there is no formal contract. However, leaving that aside, even if we accept your predecessor's terms, they do not set out the charges as you have indicated. Only if there is late cancellation is there a charge, and although one understandably loses the series discount, those terms do not indicate that the customer must repay the discount obtained earlier.'

'You have cancelled late.'

'I am sorry, but I cannot accept that. We told you of our decision more than six weeks before publication date.'

'We need to know six weeks before copy date.'

*'But that is not what your predecessor's terms state – they refer to six weeks before **publication** date. I gave you notice over three months before one publication date and over six months before the other.'*

'Well, we rely on the goodwill of our customers and I don't accept this kind of close analysis of terms.'

'But the terms govern the contract, and besides it was your analysis of these terms which led to this discussion. That analysis was totally incorrect, hence our querying it. I repeat that we have given several months' notice of suspension of our advert, having advertised every quarter in your magazine for several years. As a customer of some long standing I feel we are entitled to better treatment than this kind of conversation.' [3]

Key techniques

The over-riding mistake the caller made was to assume that she either did not need to check the terms or knew them better than the person she was phoning bearing in mind she had full knowledge of the subject matter, had initiated the call and thus held the initiative. When it became obvious that there was a disagreement regarding the terms it would have been preferable for her to have said that she would check the position and come back to the agency rather than trying to bluff it out.

1 It is unlikely if this is the best method of talking to a long term advertiser and customer.

2 Angry frustration may be understandable, but is not going to solve the problem, it will simply make a poor situation worse. Seeking to obtain sympathy as a technique seems curious, but is surprisingly widespread. It is rarely effective.

3 If debating or relying on terms then

   a it is essential that there is complete understanding of their import,

   b that the terms are actually applicable, and

   c that they are quoted correctly. Losing one's temper, for whatever reason, will almost certainly result in losing the argument. Far better if 'caught on the hop' to say, 'Sorry there seems to have been some misunderstanding here, I must consider this and will come back to you.'

Note: Looking at the conversation from the agency's angle, they felt, having checked the position regarding the terms (which obviously the magazine representative had not) that they could afford to be flexible concerning the application of the terms. Hence they could respond placidly to comments that became increasingly heated on the other side – possibly being aggravated by the caller's realisation that she was in the wrong and unlikely to win this tough call. It would have been better to have accepted and apologised, and even offered the adverts at a cut price to avoid cancellation. Handling tough calls positively and innovatively may mean we can still rescue something from them. Losing with a bad grace will never win anything (not even respect).

d Who was at fault?

e Do we need to apologise?

f Is our position defensible?

■ if so, how is it best defended without being aggressive?

■ if not, what's the worst case and how do we avoid it?

g Should we have foreseen what happened?

h What sort of recompense is needed

■ time?

■ inconvenience?

■ expense?

i Does this have potential effects elsewhere?

j Does it have a public relations dimension?

k What precedent(s) could this create?

l What is my scope/authority?

m Do I have power to deal and/or negotiate?

n Am I prepared to deal and finalise this matter here and now?

o Would I prefer time to think?

p Are there legal ramifications and if so do I need advice?

q Do I have any clinchers, trump cards, unexpected items to use to gain my desired result if things do not go well?

7 Administration

a What happens if they are not there?

b Should I compose a message in readiness to be left?

c Do I want them to ring back or would I prefer to hold the initiative in making the call?

8 Follow up

a At end of call recap

- what we have agreed,

- what we have left without agreement,

- who is going to do what.

b What have I to do?

c When must I do it by?

d What have they agreed to do?

e When by?

9 Sundries

a Did I listen to what was said?

b Did I hear anything further?

c Did attitudes change during discussion and, if so, why?

5

■ ■ ■

Some tricks of our trade

Key learning points

1 Determining common failings may indicate ways in which we can improve our performance and success.

2 Developing some basic tricks of the trade may help us win more tough calls than we lose.

3 SARAH can help focus our attention on the essential ingredients of a successful call (successful being one where toughness is avoided or evaded).

4 Getting the basics right can also assist timing, mode of address, ensuring it is the right person at the other end, and so on.

Developing our own tricks
■ ■ ■

True communication involves both parties speaking to each other and, by using feedback and explanation, each achieving an understanding of what the other says and means. It does not of itself mean they will agree, but at least if communication has taken place at this basic level it should mean that there is an understanding of each other's points of view. However, in reality we need to bear in mind the point made by the US research which indicates that only around 11 per cent of our message will get through when we use the phone as an (imperfect) means of communication as well as the general research that indicates that we are likely to remember only around 20 per cent of what we hear anyway.

In many ways, therefore, other than calls where there is purely information to be conveyed, no call that is made is likely to be straightforward and indeed, in view of the foregoing, we should regard all calls that we make as essentially and potentially 'tough'. All is not lost, however, since the realisation of this fact provides us with a considerable advantage; after all if we are anticipating toughness we can prepare for it. In Case Study 4.2 the shop assistant should have suspected something was amiss simply because the customer was making the call. He was hardly going to waste time and money stating that it had arrived safely; the very fact of the call was a sure indication that something was wrong. This very fact should, of itself, immediately have alerted the assistant and encouraged him to be a little more circumspect with the answers to the question. The trouble is we tend to think of things from our own point of view rather than from that of the other party and also to assume that we know more about them than someone who has only become involved once 'because we deal with these matters all the time don't we?'.

In the interests as much of self-preservation as winning tough situations it may be advisable to develop some tricks that will enable our calls (and/or our defences) to be more effective:

1 *Using common sense* – although our education system may teach practical subjects such as cookery and fitting a plug top as well as academic subjects, including writing English, rarely is there any advice either at this stage in a person's life, or later on, on how to use the phone (that is using the language colloquially) or even setting out the problems highlighted in this chapter so that at least we are aware of them. This is so, even though for many, the phone may (apart from talking face to face) be the most used method of required contact in their working lives – many people pre-ferring to phone than to write since they believe their writing skills to be inadequate – a 1995 survey indicated that as many as 90 per cent of the population feel their lit-erary skills to be inadequate. However, the thought that verbal skills (both in use of basic language and in communi-cation) may also be inadequate, tends to be overlooked. The trouble with common sense is that consideration of its use seems to indicate that it is not that common at all and some of the items put forward as sense are pretty nonsensical.

Case study 5.1

OH GREAT!

The sole trader got back to his office to find his answerphone 'message received' sign flashing. However, on playing it, he found that the machine had developed a fault and no message had been recorded. The next day he received a letter from a supplier which stated *'thank you for your enquiry of [date] in response to which we left a message on your answer-phone yesterday.'*

Key technique

Nice, sound idea to confirm in writing that a message had been left since machines can go wrong. But wouldn't common sense have dic-tated that if you are going to take the trouble to write concerning the matter that it might have been more sensible, to have set out the message in the letter as well. As it is the trader has a non-message on the machine and another non-message in his hand – a complete information failure – let alone a communication failure.

2 *If we wish to use a system which provides instant access we must be ready and able to provide the instant response.* Failure to meet this essential challenge is a fundamental reason for the creation of many awkward calls. By providing the facility to phone we create the perception that we are ready to respond instantly, if we are not then we fail to satisfy the demand we have actually created.

Case study 5.2

AND THEY ARE IN THE BUSINESS OF COMMUNICATION?

During a burglary a mobile phone was stolen. Concerned in case the thieves used it to the phone company's cost, the subscriber rang the phone company. After several rings an answerphone message informed him how much the company valued its customers and wanted to answer his call but they were very busy and he was in a call stacking queue. After 20 seconds of irritating music, the same voice gave him the same message. He tried four times on day one, five times on day two and twice on day three – all with the same result. On one occasion he hung on for five minutes – only to hear the voice tell him over 20 times how much they valued their customers! This was a company in the communication business.

Key technique

Mean what you say. If you are in the communication industry you need to be better at communications than everyone else or your credibility sinks below zero.

Note: In this instance the music was quite pleasant. Care should be taken in choosing pieces of music for this purpose. One well-known consumer goods company previously used 'The Sting' without, apparently, realising the somewhat unfortunate connotations such a piece of music might conjure up in the minds of callers.

3   *Thirdly, and perhaps most importantly, familiarity may breed contempt.*

Case study 5.3

NICE CALL – SHAME ABOUT THE MESSAGE!

To the current generation using the phone is second nature to such an extent that it is used without thinking – indeed listening to one's own children carry on a conversation may provide an insight into why, despite it being such a valuable aid to business, the telephone is often poorly used or used with such poor communication results.

The teenager seized the phone to call her friend for a chat, despite the fact that it was only hours since they last met when they walked home from school together. After 30 minutes when her parents, concerned at their rapidly escalating phone bill, suggested enough was enough, she eventually rang off. Only to exclaim as she took her hand from the handset *'Oh, I meant to ask her about so-and-so'*. In the eagerness to place the call, its main purpose had been overlooked.

Key technique

Whilst a little (over the top) OTT for a private call like the above, a list (even if only a mental one with a concentration on the number of points required to be raised) should help the progress of the call and avoid disturbing the respondent again when the forgotten item resurfaces in our recollection.

Each of these case studies has a lighter side but the problems they highlight are serious: inadequate preparation, lack of problem appreciation, even a basic failure to achieve communication at its lowest level. Not for nothing did Tom Peters (author of *In Search of Excellence* and *The Excellence Challenge*) comment that the only magic of the $40 billion giant IBM in a $500 billion industry was that they happen to be the only company that ever answers its phone!

4 *Fourthly, we need to ensure we can manage change.* In dealing with (or avoiding) tough calls, the phone user's responsibility is to manage or bring about change from the *status quo*, since if there is an awkward encounter there must already be a degree of disharmony. Since human beings are essentially creatures of habit, change can often be extraordinarily difficult to effect. There is an instinctive resistance to change which can be exacerbated by pride. Being prepared to acknowledge that one is in the wrong is exceedingly difficult for many people and impossible for some, for example the shop assistant in Case Study 4.2.

One is reminded of the heartfelt plea of Oliver Cromwell when addressing the General Assembly of the Church of Scotland 'I beseech you, in the bowels of Christ, think it possible you might be mistaken', which might be a suitable slogan for all those placed in the position of trying to defuse an awkward situation – the 'you' in this case being ourselves as much as anyone else. If we feel we are dealing with a closed mind we need to examine our own mind to ensure that it is open and receptive. In *Parallel Thinking* Edward de Bono argues that Western thinking (based as it is on the precepts originated and perfected by orators in classical Greece) fails our modern society because it tries to put all decisions into boxes – that is to categorise everything. In view of the rapid (and increasing) rate of change, it is, de Bono argues, impossible to categorise everything in this fashion. This is an attitude into which we can become trapped particularly when dealing with repeated situations. Because they appear similar we may be trapped into assuming they are the same. Because we now perceive them to be the same, we feel that it is appropriate that we can provide the same response as we did previously. But since no two situations are ever the same (if only because the caller at the other end of the phone is different) if we try to use a standard response all we may do is to exacerbate the situation. This is particularly a problem for those who deal with requests many of which they believe to be false. There is a danger of becoming over-suspicious and treating genuine complainants or enquirers with the same suspicion which can verge on the hostile turning the enquirer into an angry complainant.

5 *Anticipating response.* In dealing with tough calls we are faced with the problem of calculating and anticipating human response. In this the onus for success lies on us, since our initial actions and attitudes are key to such responses. Often our own attitude is key to the development of the awkward call. Although, for example, our tone may become conditioned by the responses, initially we should set the tone for the encounter. If our attitude is negative and critical, then almost inevitably the instinctive response will be defensive and resentful, and no rapport will be created between the parties, ie the negative approach creates a negative response. The person with a genuine query who receives a reaction which is suspicious (borne of experience) will understandably resent such an attitude in view of their own (perceived) strong case. This is a recipe for disaster.

Conversely, if our attitude is helpful (despite everything – and everyone – that has gone before) and we are prepared to listen (really listen to what is said and is not said) and to deal with the matter as a one-off, similar though it may be to many other calls, then we stand a very good chance of avoiding the worst of the awkwardness, indeed even of avoiding any awkwardness.

Lee Iacocca, the man who saved the Chrysler Corporation from liquidation, once said 'It is important to talk to people in their own language. If you do it well, they'll say: "God, he said exactly what I was thinking". The reason they're following you is that you are following them.'

The critical requirement in any potentially confrontational situation is the realisation of the other party's viewpoint and assessment of 'loss' or required reaction. As previously mentioned, the retention of an open mind on this subject is essential. Sadly, this assessment of the other party's viewpoint and anticipated reaction requires a depth of understanding and perception which experience indicates is possessed only by a minority. We need to determine and then exploit all the advantages or possibilities that seem to give us an edge in order to ensure we are most likely to achieve success. This may require us to be creative in our approach to the problem.

Case study 5.4

SWEET SMELL OF SUCCESS

It is said that the most retentive and evocative of our senses is the sense of smell – smelling a familiar scent can instantly transport us (at least figuratively) to the scene where last we found that smell. Using this knowledge at least one pre-war publisher used to publish detective novels with tangible 'clues', for example scented pages designed to enhance the imagination of the scene of the 'whodunit'. More recently, credit card organisations have experimented, with some success, in sending to those with a poor payment record, statements impregnated with an aroma which, when smelled, generates fear. It is reported that an increased number of those who received the smelly statements settled their bills promptly than was the case with those sent accounts which had not been so treated!

Unfortunately so far we cannot release aromas at the other end of our telephone connection that will bring sweetness and light to our tough calls or guarantee our own success. Nevertheless, there are things that we can do which will enable us to set up our calls in such ways that we may stand a better chance of success.

SARAH – key principles leading to better communication and fewer tough calls
■ ■ ■

Anyone who has to interface with people (whether face to face, or more importantly, in this context, over the phone) needs guidance and assistance. Although it is probably true that the best communicators and leaders are born, all of us can practise to improve. The principles of good direct communication and interfacing can be summed up in the process described by the mnemonic SARAH. SARAH is a friendly and helpful export from the USA and, although she was originated for use more in selling, her principles apply equally to all one-to-one relationships.

Smile and stop talking

Whilst it may be difficult to give the impression of a smile over the phone – basically if the attitude is pleasant and helpful most people are likely to respond. Equally we should be prepared to listen. Nothing riles most people more than for the other party to keep talking, preventing them putting their point. It seems that an attempt is being made to 'talk out' the subject matter. A 'smiling' or informal approach relaxes most people and can have unexpected results.

Case study 5.5

SMILE – AND SELL

In writing information updates for a publication I once invited readers to telephone for an explanatory handout. Forgetting that if it is free you tend to be inundated with requests, I did not ask for any payment. When about the fiftieth caller rang for the handout, I saw the funny side of it and we had a good laugh about my mistake. At the end of the conversation he commented that it was very unusual to hear laughter on the phone. I replied that I thought that was a pity as it was a great way of creating a rapport, and in any event why shouldn't business be fun, after all we spend a great deal of our waking life working. Eventually I sold a couple of books to him!

The use of laughter is under-rated. In the nursery a baby laughs around 450 times a day. Sadly the average adult laughs only around 15 times a day often because tradition suggests that certain things need to be treated with a degree of seriousness. Whilst not suggesting we should trivialise matters, regarding everything as unduly serious can help no-one. In inviting comments on seminars, many delegates' responses suggest that most people prefer a little lightheartedness and controlled humour to leaven the working day.

It should not be overlooked that smiling actually relaxes your vocal cords and very often the fact that you are smiling will actually communicate itself to the caller. Because your vocal cords are relaxed your tone will be relaxed; because you are relaxed they are more likely to be relaxed and a rapport is more likely to be created. In turn this should avoid or defuse a tough call. If you don't believe this is true try listening to some of the best broadcasters on the radio whose approach as far as a positive telephone manner may well be emulated. One of the best loved was Brian Johnston whose commentaries (on life as much as on the game), were to both cricket lovers and others a delight since you could appreciate the delight and humour in his tone. Both helped create a rapport between him and his listeners.

Active listening

The corollary to ceasing to hammer home one's point of view to the exclusion of that of the listener is to listen more. Hearing is a purely mechanical act, whereas listening entails active consideration of what is both said and left unsaid. Only if we listen to both what is and is not said will we gain the real views of the other party. The longer people talk the more they reveal of their true feelings – this may mean that conversations must last longer – but the pay off may be more productive calls.

Repetition of content

To show that the caller (or respondent) has understood exactly what the respondent (or caller) has said they should repeat key sentences or comments in their own words. This has four advantages:

- it helps fix the details of the matter in the mind;

- it helps check that what has been received was what was meant;

- it engenders a rapport and understanding between the two parties; and

- it leads to really accurate communication (that is the accurate comprehension of the points by both parties).

Act with empathy

This entails showing the caller that you understand and appreciate the feelings and motivation of the respondent. Obviously this will not be necessary in all cases but many tough calls can be defused if the other party understands the problem and can only be exacerbated if it is plain that they do not.

79

Case study 5.6

EVERYTHING'S COMING UP ROSES

The customer had ordered some roses for St Valentine's day. When, late in the afternoon, they had still not arrived he rang the store. The telephonist could not have been more helpful and considerate and her concerned attitude (appreciating that the flowers arriving even one day late lost the point of the gesture) went a long way to defusing what was a potentially tricky call requiring at least a refund and potentially compensation.

Key technique

One wonders how many respondents would have been able to deal with a problem so positively? Contrast 'bored voice' in Case Study 6.3.

Handle with care

Handle the subject matter with appreciation of the feelings of the other party which we can do only if we try to place ourselves in their position. If we do this, it may force us to modify our approach with resultant success.

Getting the basics right
■ ■ ■

Timing

Reference has already been made to the need for consideration for the respondent in terms of the timing of a call. If we
want to win, the best chance we have is of speaking when
the respondent is not under pressure. If we try and raise an
awkward subject when stress is present we stand a better
than even chance of not achieving our aim.

Case study 5.7

TAKEOVER

The predator had built up a small stake in the target company which
had not gone unnoticed. It was hardly any surprise when, last thing one
dark Monday in December, the company secretary received a telephone
call from a public relations firm which he knew only by name asking
questions regarding the company's share register. Basically, the
enquirer wanted a copy of the register without needing to visit the company's out of town registrars, but instead of making this request in a
polite tone he stated

'Do you know this is the fifth time I've phoned you today.'

'I'm sorry but I have no record of outstanding calls.'

*'I didn't believe you'd phone back so I didn't leave my name – I've been
chasing you all day – you've really held me up.'*

*'I'm sorry but firstly I am busy and this is an exceptionally busy time of the
year, and secondly since I didn't know you had called there was nothing I
could have done. I always ring callers back as soon as possible but if they
are not prepared to leave their name there is little I can do is there?'*

'Never mind that, I want a copy of your share register.'

'I see.'

'Well, are you going to give me one? I've been waiting for it all day.'

*'Mr Carter, I am sorry you have had a wasted day but that is hardly my
fault, I've been heavily involved in helping to run this company for the
benefit of the shareholders as is my responsibility, for the last 12 hours.
As for the register, as I am sure you are aware, our registrars are in*

Worthing in Sussex. You have a right to inspect the register and to take copies of entries and I suggest you do so as you could have done today, good evening.'

Key technique

Basically it was within the power of the secretary to make available a copy of the register but in view of the attitude of the caller (who forgot that he was after a favour) he could also make it difficult for the predator to obtain a copy.

Note: Fortunately the takeover bid was defeated or the secretary might have come to rue his reaction. Being in the right isn't always the safest place to be.

Respect

This means respect for the time that as a caller you are causing the respondent to lose by breaking into their day. Since you are remote you have no idea whether the call is convenient. Asking if this is so grants respect to the respondent, as well as control over the encounter. If it is not convenient then setting a time when it will be not only grants respect but may ensure when you do talk that there may be some mutual respect.

Addressing

Some people are very fussy about their title and manner of address. Indeed there is one famous story of a leading figure who having been given a Knighthood insisted that a mass of documentation bearing his name be reprinted at considerable cost simply so that he could be styled 'Sir . . .' on it rather than plain 'Mr' – as if that added anything at all to the content. This is perhaps as foolish as the caller who makes assumptions and by so doing creates a tricky call where none formerly existed.

CALL ME MADAM

An industrialist had received some research results which seemed to question some assumptions on which he had based predictions of value of a new solvent which formed part of a product he was interested in marketing. He was somewhat annoyed and decided to telephone the researcher to request that the draft report be amended to provide a more positive view. He was put through.

'Dr Sorrell' said a young female voice.

'Yes, I know it is – can I speak to him please?'

'Speak to whom?'

'Dr Sorrell of course, come on little lady, don't mess me around, I'm in a hurry. I'm Champion, Managing Director of XY Conglomerates, put me through to your boss.'

'But this is Dr Sorrell.'

82

Key technique

Hardly the best way to start a conversation during which it was hoped that an opinion would be subject to change. Basically on the phone one never knows who one is speaking to. Assumptions can be very dangerous as well as, as here, being patronising, insulting and discriminatory.

The right respondent

It sounds as though I am stating the obvious and yet it does need to be said that when calling one should ensure that the respondent is the person we really wish to speak to. Speaking to the wrong person can only land us in trouble, and can sometimes lead to the most unexpected results.

WRONG NUMBER

One company of which I was a director had a rule that telephones should never be allowed to ring – whoever was nearby should answer a ringing phone – no matter what their status. A colleague (another director) once answered a phone in the transport department and was told by the anonymous voice on the other end to *'tell Joe I've got his £50 for the last company car we sold for you'*. The subsequent investigation ended in two dismissals.

Presumably it had never occurred to the caller that directors of the company might actually be leading from the front and be out and about on the shop floor at the sharp end!

The authority (as well as the voice) of the organisation

When we make a call on behalf of our organisation we actually represent that organisation. We are, during the call, the face (or at least the voice) of the organisation. It may even be easier for us to give such an impression than if we are dealing face to face with the other party. There is such a thing as a telephone manner which we tend to adopt to greater or lesser extent. This can be misleading and we need to ensure that we do not give the impression that we have greater authority than the level that we do have.

83

'You keep me hanging on'

This is one of the cardinal sins of phone calls, and one of the easiest ways to create an awkward call, or make a tough call even tougher. When we are waiting, time seems magnified. Not only may we be wasting our caller's time if we keep them hanging on, but we are also sending them a semiotic message – *'your time is not as valuable as mine so you can wait there until I find the answer'*. The sensible thing is to break the conversation with a promise to ring back with the information. Having promised to do so, we need to keep that promise and make sure we do ring back.

'Ignorance is bliss'

And so, as Thomas Gray wrote, it may be, but it is one sure way of creating a tough call. Obviously it may be impossible for a respondent to know the answer to every enquiry but simply admitting ignorance helps no-one:

- the caller is no further forward;

- the respondent has been made to look incompetent;

- the semiotic message is *'I don't know and if truth be told I don't care very much'*;

- aggravation is likely to increase.

Having said that it is infinitely preferable to state that you do not know, rather than trying to flannel one's way through, which very often will become obvious to the caller in which (s)he is in receipt of a further semiotic message – *'this caller's a fool so I can con him/her with a load of old guff'*. It is hardly surprising if such an attitude backfires. It is hardly the best base to create rapport and mutual regard.

If the truthful answer is *'I don't know'* then the best answer is *'I'm sorry I am not sure about that one but I will find out and get back to you as soon as possible'*. Then of course the promise must be fulfilled as you have created an expectation.

6
■ ■ ■

'Aggravate my voice . . . to roar as gently as a dove'

Key learning points

1 Treating a caller with low importance and/or regard tends to have only one result – the creation of a situation which can become confrontational.

2 Semiotic messages can be very powerful even though they are subconscious – we need to beware these hidden messages.

3 Analysing the character and devices of potential phone users who may come our way may help arm ourselves for their tough calls.

4 Aggression should be prepared for and handled with care and firmness.

'Discretion is the better part of valour'
■ ■ ■

Avoiding the five false assumptions, giving some really objective thought to how we deal with our calls, and paying attention to the basics, should not only help us deal with awkward situations but also, and more importantly, help us avoid their incidence.

After all, if we structure it so that the person who could generate a tough call is so disarmed that he or she doesn't bother, this is infinitely preferable (as well as being far more cost-effective) to actually spending time extricating ourselves from a difficult situation. If the toughness emanates from a customer it should not be overlooked that not only is it far cheaper to retain an existing customer than it is to source a replacement but also a dissatisfied customer will spread word of their dissatisfaction far and wide. Syd Pennington, Managing Director of Virgin Atlantic, commented in 1994 that 'if someone has a bad flight he is likely to tell 17 other people' – bad news spreads like ripples on a pool and can have a cumulative effect. (If you don't believe this see Case Study 6.2 *below*.)

The more we examine the way we make and take calls the more we may observe that a large proportion which can be classified as 'bad news' can be avoided. Sometimes, however, the reverse is true – to an onlooker we seem to have set up a system designed to generate awkward calls.

Case study 6.1

SIMPLY CREATING TOUGH TELEPHONING CALLS

In October 1994 the *Sunday Times* carried a report concerning research conducted by Teleconomy, a research and training company, which had telephoned 615 branches of 20 banks and building societies. In all they made 4,500 telephone calls. Their findings to anyone believing in the value of customer care or the need to use the phone positively to serve its principles were horrific:

- only five companies had acceptable response times (which were defined as answering the phone within five rings);
- 8 per cent of the calls were abandoned when the calls were not answered within 45 seconds (15 rings).

When the call was answered:

- most staff 'spoke too fast and gave a blurred and unfriendly greeting' (obviously there were no smiles in these voices – SARAH had a day off);
- whilst handling the call and getting the right person to give the right information, not one company achieved a level of performance which the surveying organisation rated as 'acceptable'.

All too often the researchers found themselves listening to 'musak' and suffering long delays whilst their calls were transferred. In fact 12 per cent of calls were abandoned since no-one had answered after 15 rings – 45 seconds.

87

An estimated 120,000 callers to financial services providers hang up every day – an annual frustration figure of 30 million calls – fine for British Telecom, Mercury *et al*, but not for those wishing to do business with the object of those calls.

In further research conducted by the Henley Centre, although nearly half the population want to use the telephone to run their financial affairs since it can (if answered correctly)

- give immediate information,
- save time, and
- grant the customer more control,

two thirds of those asked said that the telephone service from banks and building societies was so bad they would prefer to go to a branch and deal face to face even though this would take them longer.

If this wasn't so serious it could be funny. Unfortunately, it borders on being farcical as well as foolish in the extreme. Many organisations actually encourage people to make telephone calls to them (for example by using carelines – see

Chapter Seven) since they argue that it is often cheaper and easier to deal with a telephone call than it is to deal with a letter. This is one of the principles behind the electricity company Seeboard's move towards its new systems as outlined in Case Study 7.1. However, if we are going to shoot ourselves in the foot by firstly encouraging our customers (that is the people who at the end of the day actually pay our wages) to ring us but then, when they do, treating them in a casual and totally off-hand manner, not only are we not running our business efficiently and productively, but also we will simply be creating or aggravating the incidence of tough calls as well as damaging our reputation. Reputations take years to build but can be lost in a matter of seconds.

Case study 6.2

SHOT IN THE FOOT

The classic case of a reputation being lost in seconds concerns the off the cuff remark made by Gerald Ratner during a presentation to the Institute of Directors. Ratner was at that time Chairman of one of the largest jewellery retailers in the world – he was head of a chain which he had successfully built virtually from nothing. But he humorously compared some of the products sold by his shops to human waste and added that there was more value in a Marks & Spencer prawn sandwich than in any of his products. Sales in his shops slumped, as did the share price. Ratner had to give up the Chairmanship, and later his Directorship. The name of the chain was changed and over 200 of the shops were closed. Even now, several years later, the chain has not recovered the strength and reputation it had when it was so thoughtlessly thrown away.

Key technique

When speaking on the phone the person is the embodiment of the organisation for which they work, or which they represent. This 'public voice' of the organisation should always be remembered. Poor treatment reflects not on the person but on their organisation.

The hungry competitor
■ ■ ■

There is nearly always someone else (that is some competitor) ready and willing to take our customers from us – there are relatively few genuine monopolies. In both the jewellery retailing and financial services sector for example there is no room for complacency as far as needing to attempt to better satisfy their customers. As far as financial services are concerned, any poor service does considerable damage to a reputation in particular as well as to the sector in general, which must be galling to companies such as First Direct who have conducted research which indicates that 84 per cent of its customers rate its telephone service to be better than that of traditional banks, whilst a third of its customers join because of personal recommendations from existing clients. The secret? First Direct requires its personnel to complete an eight week induction programme before anyone is allowed to take their first call. So it is possible to get it right. What we need to do is to think about what we are doing, bearing in mind that the problems highlighted by these case studies demonstrate communication problems that will create barriers quite additional to the obstructions formerly identified. The combination of barriers and obstructions is not ideal for the dual carriageway necessary for effective communication. We really have compounded the problem – and created an environment in which tough calls can proliferate.

Not such a bright idea
■ ■ ■

Although it is great that within a few seconds of picking up a phone we can be in touch with someone on the other side of the world, the fact that the reverse is true may not be so wonderful.

There are an incredible number of people who could ring us (just think of how many acquaintances and members of our families have both telephones and our private number – let alone those with whom we are in contact in business). Although it is possible to speak to more than one person at a time, few of us can really communicate effectively with two or more respondents over the phone. Equally the ability of our business to answer and deal with calls at the switchboard is limited by the number of line operators or telesales staff we have available at any one time.

Some time ago, someone realised that rather than giving an engaged signal to a caller which might mean that they don't bother to call again (in fact it is estimated that as many as 14 per cent of those who do not get through first time do not bother to call back), it might be better to answer the call and then allow the caller to hang on in a queue whilst those calling ahead of them are dealt with. On the face of it this seems a logical development of the phone as a means of communication – one can explain to the caller the situation and ask for their patience. However, what tends to be overlooked is:

1 That the caller is paying for the call. If (s)he is forced to hang on for minutes rather than seconds (as in Case Study 5.2) this can create resentment and even anger (which will understandably escalate if the subject of the call is a complaint) and we may be guilty of the equivalent of pouring petrol onto flames). This is particularly so if the caller is powerless to break out of the system.

Solutions: either

a Make the phone number a freephone – customers are more likely to hang on if they know they are not paying for the call and may then be more relaxed about explaining their problem and/or

b give the caller the initiative by inviting them either to hang on for an 'immediate' answer or to switch to another line that allows them to leave a message (see below). This gives control to the caller to determine their action rather than leaving them frustrated knowing that if they ring off they have wasted their call.

2 It is pretty insulting to those on whom the organisation relies for their lifeblood since the underlying message is 'your time is not as valuable as our time'. This may be so, but there is nothing as valuable as a customer's purchase. It is a lot cheaper to persuade an existing customer to repeat their purchase(s) than it is to source a new customer.

Solution: If you must use automatic answering ensure staffing is such that no-one waits more than 20–30 seconds.

Note: If you don't think 30 seconds is a long time – pause here and look at your watch for 30 seconds – boring wasn't it? If you didn't think so, then you may be one of the fortunate placid callers who are prepared to wait patiently. If you felt it was a long time then you are more likely to be the type who object to waiting in a queue and want to get on with things. To that type, being treated in a cavalier fashion by being kept waiting is akin to waving a red rag at a bull. Such people tend to be impatient achievers and are likely to suffer from stress and thus be more likely to respond aggressively when the phone is eventually answered.

3 What a very poor impression of customer service it gives.

Solutions:

a If costs are such that customers can be kept waiting longer than 20–30 seconds arrange that after this period an answering machine cuts in allowing them to leave a message so that someone can ring back. If this option requires the customer to state their problem this may have an added advantage in allowing someone to prepare for the call and, as has been stressed already, preparation can often defuse a potentially tough call. However, the 'call back' routine must be monitored – it should take place swiftly. Indeed, if the call back doesn't happen swiftly, it is likely to be wasted as the person may well have gone out or left the place where they can be contacted. It should not be overlooked that many people dislike talking to machines. Thus the message and its tone should be as relaxed and welcoming as possible to help overcome this antipathy. In addition, care should be taken to ensure the message is absolutely clear and unambiguous.

b Whoever answers the call eventually MUST (repeat MUST) remember that the person has been waiting for some time just to hear a human voice. A genuine and sincere apology will soften the aggravation and defuse most situations.

c Monitor when calls arrive and ensure that extra staff are available at that time.

Case study 6.3
VERY CO-OPERATIVE

Co-op Bank's Armchair banking keeps records of all incoming calls and noticed peaks between 10 and 11 on Monday mornings and between 4.30 and 5.30 each afternoon. Monitoring demand enables them to try to ensure additional staff are available to minimise delay.

4 That it may be dangerous to rely on the technology – sometimes it breaks down and the caller finds that they are no longer in the queue at all but the 'machine' has disconnected them. If they still wish to pursue their call, (remember that 14 per cent give up at this point) then, at their own expense, they will have to redial and no doubt join the queue further back than they were before. What a really great way to create a tricky call where none existed previously!

Human preferences and failings
■ ■ ■

In *An Essay on Man* Alexander Pope said that the 'proper study of mankind is man' and we can adapt that quote to suggest that in studying the use of the phone and its derivatives (particularly in tough call situations) we should study primarily its users.

The 1994 in-depth study of the use of the phone conducted by the Henley Centre already referred to, assessed the phone's potential for business. The study noted that the phone and its technology has now reached critical mass in the UK so much so that those who use the phone have confidence in such use and are prepared to use it more. This is hardly surprising given that many people believe their verbal skills to be better than their literary skills and feel more confident in making contact verbally than in writing.

There is also a feeling, which is quite widespread, that letters (particularly letters of complaint) can be, and often are, ignored by organisations whereas having a contact on the end of the phone is likely to be more effective – 'there is someone there who I should be able to pin down and make understand' runs their reasoning. In addition ours is an impatient and apparently increasingly assertive, even aggressive, society, and more and more want immediate action which it is felt is more likely with the phone than with alternative means of communication. The Henley report, however, highlights the fact that business has not yet caught up with the trends in using the phone and does not always handle the results properly. Hence the increasing number of organisations who rely on their callers being prepared to hang on until they can be dealt with by employees who are obviously inadequate (in number – and sometimes also in skills and experience) for the demands placed upon them. Not content with insulting callers in this way (what is happening is that the organisation is sending a semiotic message, whether intended or not, to its callers 'you can wait – you are not as important as our other business') many organisations also subject their customers to unwanted music and often put them into a kind of telephonic maze where they are transferred from department to department, visit the same extension more than once, and are totally unable to break out of the maze to find a real human being to talk to, in order to explain their problem. The net result is aggravation where none existed before. In this way, quite literally, poor management of the calls generates (indeed ensures a proliferation of) tough telephoning. It is not good for the caller and it's not particularly good for the business either.

Making a crisis out of a drama – and losing business
■ ■ ■

It is very odd that having invested so much capital in efficient, state-of-the-art equipment and projecting a high-profile image, that many organisations pay totally in-adequate attention to the persons who are very much the first direct contact with a customer. Yet experience would indicate that, very often, the person answering the phone provides only the poorest of images for their employer and merely serves (often through their own ignorance and indif-ferent attitude) to create a tough call where none existed previously. The responsibility here is, of course, that of the organisation to provide adequate and timely training – its absence benefits no-one.

94

Case study 6.4
POOR VISION

The print on packaging becoming ever smaller, the consumer needed spectacles but disliked carrying expensive glasses when out shopping. An advertisement for folding glasses seemed to solve the problem and he telephoned an order, paying by credit card. Nothing was heard for eight weeks although the customer noticed that the amount had been debited from his credit card account.

On telephoning the company, the bored voice of a young girl mumbled the question *'Was the magnification 3 dioptres?'* After requesting the sentence be repeated twice as he couldn't understand what was being said, he confirmed this was so, and was then told that they were still awaiting delivery which was expected *'very soon'*. He asked why, in that case, had the supplier (non-supplier more accurately) debited his credit card account six weeks previously. *'That's for security – we can't leave cheques lying around here.'* *'But this is an Access debit.'* Silence. At this point not a single word of apology for the delay had been offered, and the message being conveyed in fact, if not in intent, was *'can't really be bothered with you'*. Accordingly, getting this message, the customer continued *'Well, as you are obviously not particularly concerned about the matter, I'll make it a bit easier for you, please cancel my order.'*

Even in agreeing to do that, 'bored voice' had to be reminded that as well as the customer's name and address they would want the credit card account details in order to refund the amount taken.

Result: One lost order, one set of costs with no revenue, one dissatisfied customer and one potentially adverse public relations sore, where a little courtesy and apology (neither of which cost anything) could have won the day. Tough call score: Customer 1 Supplier 0 (in fact less than zero as it will have borne costs and has nothing to show for those costs and in addition has damaged its reputation).

Key techniques

1 Ensure all telesales personnel are monitored for helpfulness and customer care.

2 Always apologise (even where unnecessary) as it aids rapport between the two parties to the call and, besides which, most people find it very hard to maintain annoyance or temper when the other party is apologetic.

3 Be alert and understand the customer's viewpoint.

95

Note: In fact this company redeemed itself by means of a personally telephoned apology from the Managing Director who undertook to ensure such a poor advertisement for his company was not repeated. 'Bored voice' should not be blamed out of hand as obviously she may not have had the benefit of a proper training programme, or, if she had, her performance was not being monitored by supervision. Having said that, one would have thought that simple basic courtesy could have overcome much of this problem encounter.

An alternative scenario

The curious thing about the situation recounted in Case Study 6.4 is that the company had placed advertisements in the national press to generate business, yet was prepared to lose such business by poor execution of the orders it wanted to win. The other, and very sad, fact about the situation is that this casual treatment of a customer is by no means unique. How much more preferable would have been the following alternative script.

'Bloggs Mail Order company – Jackie speaking – can I help you?'

'I placed an order on 24th August, have heard nothing and find you have already debited my credit card account with the cost.'

'Could I have your name, sir, and the product you ordered?'

'Mr Robinson and the order was for a pair of triple-magnification folding spectacles.'

'Oh, I am so sorry Mr Robinson, we had such a demand as a result of that advertisement that we used all our ready stock and our reserve stock and are waiting for the replacement stock which should be in any day now.'

'Well why have you debited my credit card account?'

'That's for security reasons – usually we aim to despatch the goods within seven days of making the debit but this time we got caught out by the demand. I am so sorry you have been kept waiting but we should be able to despatch the glasses within the next seven days, or else we can refund the charge to your credit card account today, whichever you would prefer.'

Key techniques

1 Using her own name as well as that of the customer creates a rapport between assistant and customer and helps defuse the aggravation that could well be bubbling beneath the surface – the customer already has a grievance so the aim must be to mollify him, not to turn a grievance into a dispute.

2 A crisp business-like response provides an impression of efficiency. Since the response is business-like this immediately puts pressure on the caller to treat the matter in the same way rather than losing his temper at such apparent poor service.

3 Use of the term 'sir' acknowledges the relationship between the two parties – ultimately the customer is in control.

4 The obvious knowledge of the reason for the problem also aids rapport with the customer. Nothing irritates customers more than raising a problem only to find that the other person knows nothing of it, and it is impossible to be put through to someone who does. Ignorance aggravates frustration and demands.

5 The immediate apology should mollify all but the most annoyed and potentially tricky customers.

6 Offering the customer the choice of money back or waiting a little longer returns to the customer complete control of the encounter. If this had been the instant response, in all probability the order would not have been cancelled and despite the original discourtesy, the sale would have been preserved.

Service does not equate to subservient
∎ ∎ ∎

97

Whilst we in the UK tend to be characterised by a lack of aggression until aroused and a willingness to compromise, we also tend to have a very odd attitude to service. Relatively few see the provision of good service as an end in itself. It is almost as if in seeking service we feel we will be requiring subserviency.

Service is all about providing value for money, which should be what we aim to do all the time in making and taking calls. In business we certainly should not wish our staff to be subservient but we should insist they provide good service. Of course, this is only likely to occur if our staff are (unlike, presumably, 'bored voice' in Case Study 6.4) well-motivated and positive. One solution to avoiding tough calls is to ensure that those whom we require to deal with them, are themselves well motivated and the guidelines set out below may be apposite.

Motivating the tough call fielders

1 Clearly define and set the tasks for the team (using unambiguous and clear language) and coach and support those required to achieve it.

2 Actively manage (i.e. support, coach, train, develop) the team members – particularly if they become involved in a tricky call. It may defuse the whole situation if a more senior person takes control of the problem.

3 Talk to and, even more importantly, listen to each member of the team – especially if they have problems.

4 Delegate (or empower) to as great an extent as possible so that you (as manager) can stand back, plan for the future and spend time with individual team members.

5 Discuss problems and use suggestions and ideas from those involved.

6 Resolve existing, and then outlaw future, demarcation disputes.

7 Draw solutions from team members rather than imposing solutions on them.

8 Be visible, approachable, and patient.

9 Try to ensure the disliked tasks (eg dealing with calls that tend to develop into 'toughness') that have to be done are shared out – and it will aid the creation of team spirit if the team leader does his/her fair share of such tasks. Team members should be:

- known by name (preferably with details of background and home life and concerns also known);

- treated as responsible human beings capable of rational thought;

- led to clearly defined aims and tasks;

- involved in planning and improving work processes;

- provided with support, assistance and guidance as and when required;

- praised as well as criticised when appropriate;

- encouraged to take on more responsibility (but only if they want this);

- trusted to be able to deal with bad news responsibly.

Checklist of suggestions for means of motivation

1 Since the motivational effect of the average pay rise is said to last around three months, logic might suggest that smaller but more regular rises might aid motivation rather than one annual increase. The effect could be more beneficial if such rises were unexpected and related to special effort or achievement.

2 Recognition of special achievement by regular awarding of a trophy to be displayed at the appropriate workplace until it is awarded elsewhere. Peer recognition can be a powerful motivator.

3 Allowing flexible working arrangements subject to certain rules (eg *re* core time that must be worked, and maintaining adequate records of time worked – and work done).

4 Awarding additional/new benefits such as private health care/screening, social events and family days, a discount scheme with local businesses, counselling services. (It must be stressed that such benefits can only be GIVEN once – and once given it can be extremely difficult to remove them.)

5 Allowing/encouraging employees to participate in secondments or charity/voluntary working – possibly on a day a month basis rather than block absence.

6 Sponsoring training both in organisation time and employee time for qualifications that may not necessarily be directly related to the work of the organisation.

7 Inviting employees to suggest ideas which they think would improve their own motivation. Involvement tends to generate commitment.

8 Assistance financially either short term – with unexpected/ pressing commitments, or long term *via* mortgages, etc.

9 Changes to the workplace/working practices that will result in a more pleasant environment – this may also be less stressful which may provide benefits in other directions.

10 Participation in ownership of the employer – if employees can relate to something as their own they will become more

personally involved in it, protecting its business and its reputation.

NOW IT'S MINE

The company had introduced an employee share ownership and was pleased that in the first year around 70 per cent of the employees had qualified for, and been allocated, shares. The Director noticed an increasing trend away from the mad rush to leave the building at 5.30 to a more leisurely and spaced leaving – and an improvement in team spirit throughout the organisation. When the switchboard closed anyone left could field incoming calls. When one day he was beaten to fielding a call he was intrigued to find who had collected the call and went into the general office to find the cleaners' supervisor chatting on the phone. Tactfully listening to the call he heard her give accurate details of one of the company's main products and suggest that if she took his address she could arrange for a brochure to be sent to him. When she completed the call he complimented her on her handling of the query – *'I thought I was the only one here'*, she replied *'and I didn't want us to lose a sale.'*

7

. . .

Keeping the customer satisfied

Key learning points

1 Dealing with a customer's tough calls is likely to be less costly than dealing with their correspondence, but we must set up the right procedures to deal with such calls.

2 Those manning carelines must care and need to be properly trained – not only in people and communication skills but in product knowledge, etc.

3 It is essential that in dealing with customer queries the exact problem is identified and a DARNing process instituted.

4 Doing a deal over the phone can resolve the problem swiftly and economically and may avoid creating a precedent as there is nothing available as evidence.

Staff care
■ ■ ■

It is essential that those required to deal with tough calls are themselves well motivated so that they in turn deal positively with callers. Basically only if the employee is committed to the employer is such commitment likely to be in turn bestowed on the caller. The attitude of the respondent in Case Studies 5.6 and 6.5 can be contrasted with that in Case Study 6.4 – the former employees (despite one not being involved in sales at all) gave excellent service and were ideal ambassadors for their employers – the latter was anything but. If the employer 'cares' for the employees then those employees are more likely to care for the customers who help pay their wages.

This whole question of customer care revolves around treating those who pay our salaries in at least the way we ourselves would like to be treated – particularly on the phone. This problem quite rightly receives far more widespread attention than it used to do. The emergence of consumer protection organisations as well as changes in the law itself, requires that organisations that value their reputation (and their purse) should try to ensure that they 'keep the customer satisfied'. Indeed, in the UK and in Europe, in view of the shrinking of demand as a result of the worldwide recession of the early 1990s, simply trying to retain customers is a factor of economic survival. The loyalty of such customers will only be retained if they are satisfied – there is usually another supplier (and sometimes more than one) well able to grab the business if they become dissatisfied with our performance. Tony Palmer, chief executive of construction giant, Taylor Woodrow, was quoted in late 1995 as saying that a good corporate image can make customers between 1 and 5 per cent more willing to buy – often enough to tip the balance in a company's favour. Taylor Woodrow is starting to train its 8,500 staff to enhance the company's image by doing and saying the right thing. 'We need all our staff to understand public relations,' he said.

Adequate training must be provided for all employees interfacing with customers and nowhere is this need more keen than for those placed in the position of taking and making tough calls with customers. Above all what needs to be explained to employees is that unless the organisation satisfies its customers and keeps them satisfied then fairly soon they (the employees) could cease to be employed. Unfortunately this realisation that the continued payment of everyone's wages is totally dependent on customer satisfaction is often overlooked, and may be countermanded by a defensive reaction to legitimate customer query or complaint.

This reaction to customer query is widespread in the UK and at variance to reactions on both the Continent and the USA. This is not to imply that the customer is always right, sometimes complaints are unjustified and unreasonable, and must be resisted. Very often, however, observations are denied in a totally unreasonable way. Regardless of the correctness or otherwise of the complaint, the person dealing needs to use tact and diplomacy and, as has been stated repeatedly, to have all the facts immediately to hand.

103

Listen, listen, listen
∎ ∎ ∎

As has already been stressed, only if we listen very carefully to what is being said can we even start to deal with a tough call. If you really understand what someone is saying (and why they are saying it) you have gained information you may not have had before. However, no-one can understand unless they listen very carefully as much to what the caller does not say, as to what they do say and how they say it. It can be difficult to listen positively and to think at the same time – thus pausing before replying is essential to ensure that everything is taken in. If anything there is the slightest hint of a lack of clarity then remember the R in SARAH (see

Chapter Five) – repeat the content: 'can I just check that I understand you correctly, are you saying that . . .' and don't be pressurised into an instant response. If necessary say you will ring back – or in the last resort cut yourself off – anything to gain thinking time!

DARN
■ ■ ■

In my book *Dealing with Demanding Customers* I referred to the mnemonic DARN. The process and concept of darning in needlework is to repair and make as new, and this is the underlying message of the mnemonic in this context. When there are problems with customers, there's a break in the fabric of supplier and purchaser. Thus DARN stands for **Dis**covery, **A**pology, **R**ectification and **N**ovation which identifies the four stages of the process by which we hope to 'de-toughen' our calls from customers and to repair the sales 'fabric'.

1 By listening hard and asking open questions we seek to get the facts down so that we can **D for D**iscover and identify the problem experienced by the caller.

2 Assuming this indicates that we as the supplier (in the widest sense of the word) are at fault (and even if we are not or the possibility of fault is unclear) this should generate at a very early stage in the telephone call an **A for A**pology. Apologising can draw the sting from most such calls, whereas people can lose their temper when faced with intransigence, when the other party is apologising most people warm to them and lose their anger – rather than their temper. It can be difficult to maintain anger or annoyance when the other party seems genuinely sorry and is, apparently, trying to rectify the matter.

3 This brings us to the next stage in the process – **R for R**ectification. Since the supplier is at fault (and even if sometimes we are not, since it can be counter-productive to argue) we need to make amends in some way. In this, using the telephone (see Case Study 7.1) to deal (and in

reality 'do a deal') with the caller can be very useful since we are not committing ourselves to paper and no evidence will exist for use as a precedent.

Case study 7.1

DOING A DEAL

The holidaymakers had hired a canal boat for a holiday in France. The boat, which was glowingly described in the brochure, turned out to be somewhat less appealing in reality. It also had a habit of breaking down, which it did three times meaning that instead of cruising, the holidaymakers were forced to wait for a mechanic to reach them, thus effectively wasting part of their holiday and curtailing their enjoyment. Since the mechanic commented that 'it was always happening with these boats' the holidaymakers felt this to be unacceptable.

On return, the problem was put to the cruise company which initially dismissed the complaint out of hand. Since it seemed to the holidaymaker that the company had made no effort to understand either the loss caused by the breakdowns or the ruining effect this known unreliability had had on their (and presumably other people's) holidays – he wrote to the Chairman.

The following Sunday morning he was impressed to receive a telephone call from the Chairman who, having first enquired if he minded him phoning on a Sunday, (to which he replied that he was impressed) and dealing with the problem over the phone, apologised not only for the unreliability of the boat but also for the dismissive way his initial letters had been treated. The Chairman went on to ask how they could put the damage right and it was agreed that a discount on a future holiday with the company would be appropriate.

105

Key techniques

There were a number of advantages to the company in this method of handling the problem.

1 A personal telephone call showed how seriously the company took the complaint.

2 The fact that it was the Chairman himself who made this call on what would normally be regarded as a non-working day added

solace to the 'injury' caused by the initial dismissive reaction. The company was seen to have 'put itself out', compensating in some degree for the way the holidaymakers had been 'put out' by the breakdowns.

3   The positive publicity given to this initiative had a disproportionate public relations value to the costs involved.

4   The fact that a deal was done over the phone meant as far as the company was concerned there was nothing in writing which could be quoted back to them as a basis for trying to increase the amount agreed or used as a precedent by others.

5   A deal was agreed between principals without what could have developed into a long winded correspondence which could have had the effect of further polarising viewpoints.

Remedial actions

1   Train and empower customer care employees to suggest flexible solutions to problems either themselves or by referral to supervision.

2   Try to do the deal verbally – it saves time and avoids the permanence of print.

4   Finally the darning process ends with **N for N**ovation which is all concerned with the changes we may need to make to the product, process, system, administration or whatever has been shown to be faulty. It may be that an analysis of tough calls can aid the development of whatever it is that is at fault – which is part of the theory behind the use of 'carelines' referred to below. For this reason, as well as to provide a check on quality control, details of all complaints should be regularly reviewed by senior management. If data on such problems are not reviewed and acted upon, there is little likelihood that common problems will be rectified and the incidence of tough callers will almost certainly increase, at the expense of the organisation's reputation.

Carelines

■ ■ ■

Bringing to the attention of those likely to complain, the means by which they can do so, may actually defuse a situation. Thus an increasing number of retail outlets now display signs setting out their way of attending to their customers' problems. The poor record of handling telephone calls in the financial services sector has been referred to previously and it is interesting that the Banking Ombudsman has advised banks, in view of their poor customer relations image, to display the procedure by which those who feel their treatment has been poor can lodge a complaint. Not only do these carelines advertise to those buying from, or using the services of, the supplier, the basis on which business will be conducted and their problems and concerns dealt with but also it can act as a reminder to the employees of the commitment required by the organisations.

107

Case study 7.2

TANKER TREATMENT

A private motorist was furious that a tanker 'cut him up' on a main road and indeed nearly caused a serious accident as he had to brake and swerve. Part of what is regarded as justifiable anger in such circumstances is caused by the fact that usually there is little a driver can do but swallow his annoyance – indeed that is probably the safest course of action particularly where a lorry is involved. Road rage is hardly tenable when the other party is 20 times your size and sadly there have been instances of car drivers being injured and killed when trying to make clear their annoyance at such treatment. Even if the organisation's name appears on the vehicle, there may be no easy way of contacting them, or, on contacting them, knowing whom to ask for to deal with the matter.

However, in this case, the motorist found the tanker carried a notice requesting that anyone having cause to complain about the manner in which it was being driven, should ring the telephone number displayed.

He did so and, because his call was welcomed, an apology offered and assurance was given that the matter would be taken further with the driver concerned his anger virtually disappeared.

Key technique

The very fact that he could actually report the incident to the tanker's operators played a major part in reducing his anger and the heat that could have been generated during the inevitable tricky call.

Such a 'complaint' number appears on each of the 27 lorries used by PMS International to deliver its range of 5,000 lines of toys, gifts, novelties, household goods, etc, throughout the UK. Despite the considerable mileage covered by the fleet during a year the company has received virtually no calls complaining of poor driving conduct says Public Relations Manager, John Howard.

'We are a caring organisation and feel that putting a helpline number on the vans demonstrates our commitment to all those who come into contact with our organisation, whether they are directly related to the company, like customers, or indirectly, like road users. When we put the numbers on the lorries we set up a logbook and were prepared to tape-record calls – but we've had none! We do wonder whether the fact that it is obvious that we are set up to deal with such calls, stops people from making spurious calls in the hope of gaining some advantage.'

It's an interesting idea for another way to avoid tough calls.

Many organisations are also displaying contact telephone numbers on their products and encouraging consumers to contact them with concerns, complaints or queries, recognising that by providing such a service an outlet for grievance and annoyance is provided which may take the sting out of many such complaints and also help business generally.

Case study 7.3

SMOOTH SPREADING

When rumours concerning the use of pig fat in the margarine spread Flora were circulating, many concerned Jewish consumers were able to telephone the contact number on the pack to be reassured that this was not the case.

In fact, normally Flora receives around 500 calls per week and the rationale behind setting up the careline says Mike Flipper, Marketing Services Manager, was that the company 'wanted to show that we had nothing to hide but we realised that we could learn very quickly what consumers want – they want to deal with real people'.

Whilst the main purpose of carelines is to deal with problems, those organisations that use them have realised that since they have concerned customers on the telephone they are a captive audience whose views on a whole range of matters related to the product and indeed to its competitors can be checked.

Case study 7.4
'YOU GOT IT'

BurgerKing, the fast food chain, wishing to move away from a system whereby every customer letter had to be answered in turn by letter, encourages customers to use a careline by displaying its contact number not only in-store, but even on the customer's till receipts. In dealing with the calls the company is able to derive considerable assistance in the development of its service and product range.

Key technique

Customers have valuable ideas about an organisation's products and service but few will bother to write them down. However, making a call requires less effort, is more personal, and, because views have been sought tends to defuse aggressive complaints.

A worthwhile investment?

Carelines can be an expensive investment. For example, Nintendo, the computer games specialists, spend over £50,000 a year running their telephone helpline. Despite such a service being more related to providing assistance to players of their games who have become stuck on one of the levels and are unable to proceed further, rather than dealing with more general product queries and complaint, it is possible that were it not for the existence of such lines some of their customers might have relieved their frustration by ceasing to buy their products. If so the expenditure of £50,000 (itself tiny compared to the cost of advertising their products) pales into insignificance. Some companies attempt to minimise the costs by subcontracting the service to specialist firms offering such a service to allcomers. Andrew Tillard, Managing Director of Decisions Group, a telemarketing organisation which deals with around two and a half million telephone calls from consumers *via* their freephone service, stated in May 1994 that there were then six major telemarketing companies and 50 organisations offering a careline service in the UK and estimated that the number of firms using the concept is likely to double every two years for the foreseeable future. 'The single most important factor preventing the spread of carelines in the UK is a lack of appreciation by senior managers of the importance of providing answers to customer queries,' Andrew commented in a *Sunday Times* interview. Assuming this is an accurate comment on the situation and a number of the Case Studies quoted in this book suggest this to be so, it is a sad reflection on the astigmatic nature of management's view of the importance and the power of the customer. Once again the UK may be forced to follow the example of the USA where 83 per cent of consumer goods (including all household goods) carry carelines. Research in 1994 showed that on the Continent 15 per cent of German products and 30 per cent of French products used such numbers – that is roughly twice and four times respectively the comparable figure for the UK at that time, which echoes the point made earlier that Americans and Continentals tend to expect better service than consumers in the UK. However, the trend set out above suggests that this is not likely to be the case in years to come. In the aftermath of the recession, consumers are demanding better service and better value for money. In *Managing to Survive* Sir John Harvey Jones, former chief executive of ICI and perhaps more widely known as BBC Television's 'Troubleshooter', commented 'I believe the 1990s are going to punish those who do not think about (their) problems. Your business is only as good as your customer base'. Devotees of the careline type of service suggest that if consumers who complain are dealt with swiftly and professionally (particularly on a freephone number) then it is almost certain they will become a repeat customer. Charles Weiser, head of customer relations at British Airways, endorses this point. He suggests a four point plan to convert complaining into repeating customers which can be summarised as follows.

1 Apologise and 'own' the problem. Complainers do not care whose fault it was – what they want is action and rectification.

2 Do something – and do it quickly. Initial satisfaction that something is being done, dips if customers feel they have to wait more than five days – and is destroyed if they have to ring again.

3 Assure customers that the problem is being sorted out. Those who are asked to deal with complaints must be fully aware of all that is going on – and particularly of changes in the products and services.

4 Phone them back – most customers appreciate personal service and a phone call can be more personal than a letter.

Converting complaints

Using an outside agency to field tough calls can have the effect of divorcing the customer from their supplier and may create problems, although a link by which the customer with a difficult or tricky call can be transferred to an in-company expert is a prudent fall back. In fact, such is the technology used by such lines that calls can be transferred virtually anywhere within the world and research indicates that callers do not mind being transferred providing a human voice (rather than a machine) deals with them.

Case study 7.5

THE REAL THING

Coca-Cola put a freephone telephone number on its soft drinks packaging and receives an average of just under 3,000 calls per week which raise all sorts of points, although only around 10 per cent are complaints. The company believes that its careline acts as a very good filter to indicate if there are going to be widespread problems with which it can then deal; as well as being a very good way of gauging interest in new products. When the company had problems with a sales promotion advertisement on the products the number of calls rose sharply.

Key technique

Senior management monitoring of calls is essential since this early indication of problems enables swift rectification to be instigated. Basically, a careline is a hotline to the genuine reactions of the consumers and should be used as such.

The other side of the coin
■ ■ ■

The use of a careline tends to encourage calls of which a proportion will be hoax, or useless, or even insulting and vicious. Counselling and training needs to be given to staff to try and help them cope with these kinds of calls. The response to calls which are abusive can be that the call is being tape-recorded and the number traced. This is relatively easy now *via* the use of the 1471 number remembering that details of the calls are available to the police even if the caller has previously blocked recovery of the number using this code.

Where threats or foul language are used the caller can be advised that they are committing an offence and details may be passed to the police for investigation. Under the Telecommunications Act 1984 'a person who by means of a public communication system, sends a message or other matter that is . . . menacing, or . . . causes annoyance . . .' is guilty of an offence and can be fined on conviction.

Despite such lines having these drawbacks, the value in drawing the sting from otherwise demanding customers can be immense. It is for this reason that so many formula restaurants require waiters and waitresses to enquire whilst diners are eating their main course if they are satisfied with their meal. This provides an opportunity for the diner to raise any concern, whilst, if none is mentioned, puts the restaurant in a strong position should complaints be voiced later. Conversely, not having a phone number available or any means to lodge a complaint merely aggravates annoyance into anger.

KISS and make up
■ ■ ■

In this context KISS stands for 'Keep It Simple, Stupid' and applies to a whole range of problems. It can be applied to customer care or complaint conversion since the concept is to try and ensure that explanations or interpretations, and thus negotiations or deals, do not become bogged down in needless and convoluted language and discussion. If this is important in dealing with written problems it is absolutely essential when trying to deal with tricky telephone calls as the medium simply does not lend itself to the easy discussion of complicated matters. The thrust of the KISS argument is that if we keep the whole process and the wording and understanding simple, then the scope for misunderstanding and imperfect recollection is considerably reduced. In addition, reducing matters to their simplest level, whilst avoiding any suggestions that one is patronising the other party should also reduce the time involved in the endeavour. After all, if the explanation cannot be misunderstood, further phone calls or correspondence or discussion should be unnecessary. The parties can then move to the settlement stage.

The more time spent in reconsidering matters, the more likely it is that a further edge could be discovered. If the deal is already done it becomes difficult to re-open negotiations. Often negotiations regarding customer complaints become unnecessarily complicated, resulting in positions becoming polarised, simply because too much time is allowed to pass on what can be called 'fencing' using statements and inferences all of which are capable of misinterpretation.

Case study 7.6

WHY DO THEY LET IT GET THAT FAR?

Each week in the *Mail on Sunday*, Tony Hetherington deals with consumer complaints in a series of articles called 'Questions of cash'. Using the power of the press, publicity is given to examples of (usually) poor customer relations. Whilst in some cases the consumer has misunderstood the situation and the supplying company has an acceptable explanation, very often the impact of the column is itself sufficient to prompt supplying companies to compensate, negotiate or replace where previously they were refusing to do so. Since their names are quoted, publicity is given to their 'poor' customer relationships.

Very often positions become polarised, and the original complaint obscured, because the dispute has been allowed to drag on, in some cases for years rather than days or weeks.

Key techniques

1 If the only way in which a customer can gain satisfaction is by using the power of the national press, it reflects badly on the way companies deal with tough callers.

2 Failing to foresee the potential adverse publicity is worse management than poor customer relations.

3 Often a solution is found almost as soon as a telephone call is made from the newspaper. If this is the case, why could this not have been done previously? Entrenched views and attitudes tend to cost money.

Action: Place a time limit on the solution of customer disputes at set levels of managerial intervention. For example: if a tough call is not resolved within five minutes there should be automatic referral to a more senior level of management, who should be more able to see the global situation, as well as the possibility of adverse publicity. This may encourage earlier settlement or, at least, set in place a manner by which an internal solution can be found.

Case study 7.7

PLUGGED INTO GOOD SERVICE

The recently privatised regional electricity companies have major customer-management problems. Rod Danes heads Seeboard's Customer Services department which is manned by 400 staff. Danes recognises the value of active listening: 'We're training our staff to listen to and understand what the customer is asking, not what they think the customer is asking'. Eighty five per cent of Seeboard's telephone calls are answered within 10 seconds. Consequent upon the emphasis being given to customer service the number of complaints to the Electricity Regulator is dropping rapidly.

115

Key technique

It should not be overlooked that creating and dealing with tough calls, as well as dealing with the enquiries from, in this case, the electricity regulator are time consuming and costly. Tough calls are not just annoying and frustrating – they can also be very costly.

Seeboard recognises that side by side with a different approach to customer service is a requirement for new technology. By 1997 they anticipate having installed a customer-information system based on an American system which will give staff instant access via networked personal computers to customers' full details, including their letters. Thus those dealing with the calls will have the files available to them immediately. Apart from other benefits this should reduce the length and number of such calls. Evidence can be a very effective antidote to aggravation.

Unfortunately not every consumer-orientated organisation deals so efficiently with its customer queries. Those finding fault with British Rail's error-ridden timetables in 1995 found little solace in using the telephone information service. A survey carried out by the Central Rail Users' Consultative Committee disclosed that not only were 95 per cent of the calls not answered within the promised 30 seconds, but also the information provided was often inaccurate. Although a few of the offices provided better service than others, some failed to respond to calls at all, even after repeated (as many as 20 in some instances) attempts.

It was suggested that many of the problems were caused by cutting back on staff and reducing the number of contact points. Whilst the need to reduce costs is understandable, if the result is merely to further aggravate customers this seems foolhardy in the extreme. A monopoly such as the railway network currently is may be able to survive treating its customers in such a fashion – few other organisations can afford to be so cavalier.

116

8

■ ■ ■

Dropping clangers

Key learning points

1 Preparation can make it easier to deal with tough calls –
failing to prepare simply encourages us to drop clangers.

2 Clangers (which usually 'land' on our own toes) have a
habit of reverberating and their public dimension and
backlash should never be overlooked.

3 We need to train those that have to deal with tough calls
that the interests of the callers and customer retention is
vitally important to the continuation of the organisation.

4 Positive action may be preferable to being defensive,
particularly where there is no real case to defend. Such a
negative approach will merely aggravate a situation.

The clanging syndrome
■ ■ ■

We can make it easier to minimise the effect of tough calls by:

- making preparations before we phone (or answer the phone);

- being patient with callers or respondents (which it is appreciated can be difficult if we ourselves are under pressure);

- ascertaining the facts and our desired results and trying to work towards it;

- being courteous (despite provocation); and

- making notes both of how we intend to handle the call and how it was handled (which may be two entirely different stories) so that we have a record in case there is a 'next time'.

Such an approach should reduce the incidence of 'losing' the calls, may reduce the likelihood of there being a tough follow up and should, at least, provide evidence of what was or was not agreed.

Of course, it is perfectly possible to be very courteous and yet still fail to please. Whilst organisations need to concentrate on training their staff to be polite and helpful they also need to ensure their own systems lend themselves to defusing potentially dangerous situations. Systems need to be restrictive enough to ensure control and yet flexible enough to deal with the unusual.

Part of the value of the careline concept is that it should teach us the things that those who call us do not like about the organisation and/or the way we handle our calls. Yet all too often the reality is that organisations – even those that

118

say they value their customers (such as the telephone company in Case Study 5.2) – actually pay very little attention to the needs of those customers and ignore their protests if they indicate those needs are not being met. For example, replying with a standard response to a non-standard question simply invites a tough call which is generated not only by the fact that the original question has not been answered but also because the underlying message is 'for heaven's sake here's what we have, now go away'.

Case study 8.1

CAN'T BE BOTHERED

The holidaymaker had booked with one of the UK's so-called 'leading' holiday tour operators and had experienced some very poor service which was, at least in part, compensated for by the payment of well over £100 which itself was an indication of the validity of her claim. She then pointed out that she had been overcharged for car hire arranged by the company. When no answer was received to her letter she rang the 'customer service department'.

'Did you not receive my letter?'

'Oh yes but we can't understand how you feel you have been overcharged.' [1]

'But if you have my letter you can see – I have set it out clearly. Your brochure states £104 for a seven-day hire and I have been charged £140. I accept that there is a charge for petrol to be added which could bring the amount payable to around £115 but that leaves £25 which is exactly the amount paid as a deposit to you in this country.'

'But how do you feel you have been overcharged?'

'Because the total charge should be around £115 and in fact I have been charged £140 – £25 here and £115 by debit to my credit card.'

Eventually the company sent a cheque for £25 but the customer was left with the impression either that the company employed deliberately obtuse people to man its customer service lines or they simply did not believe the point she was trying to make. The 'I fail to understand how you think that . . .' sounds like a standard phrase from the 'how to respond to difficult callers' book.

Key techniques

1 The customer could have been excused for immediately asking 'Does that mean that you simply ignore your correspondence?' If the company did not want to commit anything to writing, why not contact the customer by phone? At least it would demonstrate that something was being done.

2 Obviously some callers will 'try it on' and if there is no case then perhaps the best thing will be to state that, but if the facts are checkable and support the customer's contention it may be better to pay up and look good rather than create a poor impression by arguing and questioning the caller's veracity. At the end of the day the caller could have been an intended repeat customer.

Standard procedure

Standard responses are valuable standbys and they indicate that someone has been thinking about how to handle calls. The real problems are that:

1 the person who can devise suitable responses probably isn't around when the non-standard query pops up;

2 very often it is not a standard problem or enquiry which gets the standard (and thus inappropriate) response; and

3 the provision of standard responses can make those replying lazy so that instead of thinking and listening to the caller they trot out 'standard response Number 52'.

The whole situation can be compounded when the standard response is compounded by standard procedures which again allow no leeway to deal with out of the ordinary enquiries.

Case study 8.2

PROCEDURAL STRAITJACKET

The customer had a domestic appliance on which they had taken out a service contract with the manufacturer. The appliance developed a fault, but when the customer rang the telephone number provided on the service contract she was referred to another number with a different company.   CLANG 1

The customer rang the second number and was offered a visit five days later, although her service contract (with the original company) promised a 48-hour call.   CLANG 2

The original contract also specified that the time for the repair was to be designated by the customer 'including weekends' but this was brushed aside by the off-hand telesales staff, despite three phone calls trying to quote her contract terms.   CLANG 3

'The computer does not recognise the terms you are referring to – so the earliest available call is on Monday' was the only response.   CLANG 4

Eventually a message was left on the customer's answerphone offering a Saturday service provided she rang back to confirm she would be available at any time. On ringing back . . .   CLANG 5

. . . no-one knew anything about the Saturday offer and the customer was back to 'it's Monday or nothing' routine. At this stage the customer's patience broke and she demanded to be put through to a more senior person. This request was refused.   CLANG 6

The customer stated that unless she was put through to someone senior in the organisation she would put the phone down and her next call would be to the local Trading Standards Officer. She was put through to a supervisor who again accessed the computer and was told 'We've got you booked for Monday'.   CLANG 7

This true account reads like the screenplay for a 'customer care' disaster movie *How Not To Do It*.

The clangers leading to the tough call

1 The company had failed to notify the change of contact company and/or telephone number to the customer despite there being a legally binding contract. Whilst one can appreciate that individual notification could be costly there was a perfectly easy way of achieving the same end – an automatic switching device to reroute calls made to the old number directly to the new. In addition the consumer is hardly going to be best pleased at having to redial knowing that they've already wasted the cost of one call. Again this could have been avoided by making it a freephone number.

2 Legally, contracts can only be varied with the agreement of both parties. Increasingly consumers are aware of their rights – indeed, since 1st July 1995, all terms with consumers must be in plain English and unfair terms can be rejected by consumers piecemeal (ie they can remove one term from the contract even though the others could continue in force). Such a development opens the organisation to immediate criticism and puts it in the wrong particularly as publicity could be given to the incident.

3 Customer service must encompass customer care. 'Care' in this instance involves listening to the customer. Obviously a mistake of omission has occurred – the computer system has not been programmed to recognise older contract terms. This may be understandable, even excusable. What is neither understandable nor excusable is the casual dismissal of what the customer (ie the wage provider) is saying. Standard responses do not adequately deal with non-standard enquiries.

122

4 Staff need to recognise that, efficient as they are, computer systems are only as reliable as the staff who programmed them. The computer may not be able to make a mistake, but the human being working it certainly can. Blind reliance on the technology demonstrates a dangerous *naïveté* – 'GIGO rules OK'. ('GIGO' is short for '**G**arbage **I**n, **G**arbage **O**ut' – that is if you put rubbish into the computer you can only get rubbish out.

5 Again the customer is bearing the cost of the call – this is simply adding aggravation to an increasingly angry encounter.

6 Callers were given only the telesales service telephone number. The operators could not normally refer to higher authority. It seemed that only by becoming very angry and using threats that such reference was possible. In other words, the way the system was set up actually encouraged – almost deliberately aggravated – tough calls. Hardly the correct approach for a company claiming to provide 'good service'.

7 Referral of a call to higher authority should entail briefing of the fielder of the call with a synopsis of the background to the call. This would enable a fresh start to be made which, despite all that has gone before, might defuse an increasingly explosive situation.

Groundwork

■ ■ ■

The odd thing about the situation in Case Study 8.2 is that the problem was not complex or difficult to deal with. All it required was a little constructive thought and such confrontation could have been averted. Where there is change we do need to consider its effects from all angles and to set up systems that cater for it. Indeed, failure to do so doesn't simply create unnecessary tough calls, but hardly reflects well on our managerial capabilities. The customer in Case Study 8.2 eventually received compensation that was over twice the cost of the maintenance contract she had taken out – businesses do not need to do that very often to ruin their reputation and livelihood. A simple checklist was all that was needed.

Tough call – defusing checklist

123

1 Advise customers of any change of operator and seek approval of any change in terms.
(*Note:* This is vital in view of the change in the law already referred to regarding terms of business with individuals.)

2 Install adequate/computer records of the variations of service contract terms and warn staff that there may be variations.

3 Stress to staff that the computer is not infallible. Common sense needs to be applied to the situation.
(*Note:* In Case Study 8.2, one would have thought that there would have been a way in which the company could have requested a sight of the contract, or at least asked for further details to try and discover the real situation. As said before, common sense can be somewhat uncommon at times.)

4 If it is impossible to make the system respond to unusual situations, warn staff that they may be faced with non-standard requests.

5 To avoid needing to train all staff to deal with such non-standard requests, stipulate that all such calls be transferred to a specified contact. This could actually have been achieved by routing the calls *via* a redirect service straight to such a person.

6 Train staff to be user-friendly and to say 'sorry' repeatedly in case of dispute. For 94 per cent of people, apology can disarm complaint.

7 Provide a careline for dissatisfied customers. Hiding behind anonymity only aggravates those determined to press their claim.

8 If leaving a message, provide a contact name for response. Using a real name creates a rapport with what can otherwise be a faceless organisation.

124 The outcome of Case Study 8.2 was a letter to the Managing Director who then had to phone the customer and try to extricate his company from a difficult situation. That itself was a very tough call since the customer held all the trump cards – the Managing Director could only apologise.

Complaint checklist

Most tough calls are connected with complaints concerning faulty service or goods. Assuming the complaint is justified and inevitably some are not, the organisation needs to be on the defensive, not the offensive. It is in the wrong and it is contractually liable, and if not, legally liable and needs to bear this in mind. Whilst trying to shrug off complaints may work in some cases it is an inherently dangerous policy which can backfire and become very costly.

1 Discover the facts – customer, order, payment record, etc.

2 Listen carefully to the complaint – noting all relevant information.

3 Check any facts put forward or disputed by the customer.

4 Be courteous at all times.

5 Only if the complaint is straightforward, venture to attempt a solution.

6 In non-straightforward cases, thank the customer for bringing the matter to the organisation's attention, apologise for any inconvenience and state that the matter will be investigated.

7 Set a time limit by which the customer will receive an answer or further contact (and ensure that that time limit is maintained even if the call only requests a time extension).

8 Investigate the complaint and consider the validity of the customer's case objectively. Derive a possible response with a fall back position if the customer refuses to accept the first suggestion.

125

9 Consider any precedent that might be created from a settlement and weigh it against any potential backlash from publicity. (Although it is often said that there is no such thing as bad publicity, this is unlikely to be true where poor or faulty products can be exposed, or the safety of the consumer risked.)

10 Try to conclude the dispute harmoniously, whereby the reputation of the organisation is enhanced rather than dented.

Creating harmony

It may take more work and thought to create harmony from a tough call rather than dismissing genuinely based complaints. However, the result is at least positive and out of it may come benefits – if only the retention of a customer rather than their loss (and needing to find a replacement). In a survey of the top 200 UK companies, accountants Price Waterhouse found that less that 10 per cent analyse how many customers they lose each year even though they calculated that customer defection costs British industry about £100 billion each year, whilst a similar amount is spent on sales and distribution (that is costs incurred trying to acquire more customers!). If you lose 10 per cent of your customers each year, arithmetically you could argue that it will take ten years to lose them all. In the realities of business, unless they are replaced, it will take only about four years before you go out of business unless cutbacks are made in other areas.

Although examples of poor practice such as those in the above two Case Studies are very helpful in demonstrating actions to avoid, of vital importance is getting it right (and right first time). To level the imbalance we must also consider positive actions and reactions such as are evinced in Case Study 8.3.

Case study 8.3

SAFETY FIRST

The toy chain sold a considerable number of 'pocket money toys' – small value items which children could purchase themselves. Included in the range were a pair of scissors suitable for a small child, which were described as 'safety scissors'. A customer phoned Head Office, with a complaint regarding the scissors. His call was taken by the Company Secretary who had been alerted by the shop to which the customer had gone in order to find the name, address and telephone number of the Head Office.

'Hello, Mr Robinson, what's the problem?'

'It's these scissors your Croydon shop are selling – my son has cut his mouth on them.'

'Oh, I'm sorry to hear that – what's his name and how old is he?'

'Peter, and he was two last week.'

'Is it a bad cut – did it need stitches?'

'Well no, but it drew blood and he was upset for a couple of hours.'

'I hope he is better now . . . [1] . . . how did he get hold of the scissors?'

'They were one of the birthday presents we bought for him at your shop.'

'I would have thought two was a little young to be playing with scissors, surely children of that age tend to put everything in their mouths don't they? I know mine do.' [2]

'But the packaging states they are safety scissors so we thought they were safe.' [3]

'Well, of course, the description "safety" refers to the fact that the blades themselves have no points and both blades, except the cutting edges, which are blunt of course, are covered in plastic. As I am sure you know, unlike knives, the blades of most scissors are actually fairly blunt.'

'How can scissors be blunt – they cut.'

'They actually cut only by the scissor movement of the two blades – one against the other. With these scissors, our manufacturers protect everything else but obviously cannot stop the scissor movement otherwise they would not be scissors at all. We call them safety scissors in the same way that the manufacturers of safety pins name their pins – safety pins, although all safety pins are actually very much sharper and more dangerous than our scissors. That safety description refers to the fact that the sharp point of the pin is protected from the user – particularly important for small children and babies. Despite its name, the safety pin is sharp. Obviously despite the protection that is part of the safety pin, you would never give one to your child to play with would you?' [4]

'But surely you should put on your packaging that these scissors should not be given to young children.'

'We sell several thousand of these scissors each year and this is the first time we have heard of a cut. Obviously if there is anything we can do to avoid even a single recurrence we should examine it. I must say that we appreciate your telling us of this incident and hope that Peter has now fully recovered. What I would like to do is to send you an assortment of sweets which Peter definitely can put in his mouth, and we hope he enjoys them.' [5]

Key techniques

1   As a result of a deliberate effort the tone of the conversation is friendly and the attitude is positive. The customer's call has been welcomed and concern has been expressed at the injury, although no indication of acceptance of liability has been given. Using the name of the child tries to personalise the conversation.

2   Using a rhetorical question invites the father to agree with the statement, even though it contains an implied criticism of the family itself. Including a reference to the Company Secretary's own family tries to create a rapport regarding shared experiences and makes it clear that the ways of children and the need to protect them are known and appreciated first hand.

3 This is awkward – the double-edged question. Accepting that the ages should be on the packaging could be taken as an admission of liability, whilst dismissing it, would undermine the claim to be a responsible and sensible retailer. Care is needed in dealing with such questions/comments – and here much of the real point is ignored.

4 Using another rhetorical question gains some progress, whilst the allegation that the scissors cannot be safe has been covered by the reference to a far more widely known product also used in connection with children. Such innovative thought is very valuable in these circumstances and usually demands pre-interview consideration.

5 Without appearing too pushy, the Company Secretary seeks to conclude the call. Mr Robinson had a complaint, but the company has a reasonable defence, offering reimbursement of expenses and a small gift should settle the matter. Obviously, if it does not, then the company, mindful of the requirements of its Products Liability insurers may have to withdraw from further discussion and leave it to the insurers. Dealing with the matter by phone (rather than putting anything in writing) may actually benefit the company and its insurers as no written record remains.

General point: The fact that the call was taken by a member of senior management might itself have helped defuse the potential toughness. Giving customer 'care' senior management responsibility may, of itself, lead to a decline in its incidence and mishandling.

Conversion
■ ■ ■

It is said that there is no more passionate devotee than the person who has been converted – the smoker who gives up can often be the most virulent critic of those who continue. Similarly, the person who instigates a tough call can be converted to a fan. The call is actually an opportunity to talk to the customer. Indeed, one philosophy for dealing with tough calls argues 'give them whatever they want – but talk to them' meaning that the cost of solving any toughness may actually be worth the information that can be obtained from the conversation.

Case study 8.4

COMPLAINT CONVERSION

In the days before the introduction of the 1471 caller call back device that allows you to discover the number of the last caller (unless it has been blocked), the subscriber was being plagued by hoax and/or silent calls. He rang BT to discover whether there was anything they could do. After having discussed the problem for a few minutes the BT employee moved on to other things having by then, using the company's technology discovered the caller's name and phone records. As a result of their discussion the subscriber agreed to sign up for what was then called the 'friends and family service which provides discounts for five favoured numbers.

Key techniques

1 Whilst it is only using relatively simple technology the system whereby those being called can, with a little information (your post code), tell you your address and (with other information) even your name, does help break the ice of most calls and can help defuse a potentially tough call. It also provides an instant insight into the efficiency of the operation (see below).

2 'Whilst we are talking have you thought about . . .' may be a pretty corny conversation twist but nevertheless it is a convenient way of attempting to sell a service or product and has the added advantage of costing next to nothing – the caller is even paying for the call!

129

Efficiency – the silent weapon
■ ■ ■

If one contrasts Miss 'bored voice' and her reaction to the caller in Case Study 6.4 with the above Case Study the essential difference is that BT provided efficiency and the impression was of a representative and an organisation in control of the situation. This tends to impress and may deflate potentially tough calls. The subconscious reaction is 'well, these people seem to know what they are doing'. I have already referred to my call from Botswana and the same call can illustrate this point further. As a small operation, essentially telephone related, I set up my office in a circle with myself at its centre point. Designing the office this way means that virtually all my current files are within arm's reach. When anyone calls, without leaving my chair or putting the receiver down, I can reach most of the files and by the time they have finished their query I can often have the item in front of me. If the caller is unknown and/or unexpected it normally takes about 10 seconds for details of who they are and what they want to be assimilated by the recipient. Whether taking or making a call it is important to allow this assimilation time before moving on to the matter under discussion.

Very often the fact of having the data immediately to hand results in a surprised comment which helps break the ice and creates a rapport. Accordingly, if there is a problem or a mistake, a certain degree of mutual regard already exists which should stand one in good stead and a swift apology can immediately be built upon a sound foundation and can be very effective. It also means, like my caller from Botswana, that with an expensive call he was not kept hanging on, which can only irritate. There is nothing original about this approach but a surprising number of organisations fail in what is really a pretty basic need.

I learned this need to have instant access to data the hard way when I worked for the UK offshoot of Xerox Corporation and would get calls at all sorts of odd times from the USA. The one thing most of those calls had in common was that the caller wanted information and they wanted it NOW. Saying 'I'm sorry, I'll have to get back to you' was unacceptable. It was also (to our US parent) a poor reflection on UK managerial control – so you plan accordingly! You never get a second chance to make a first impression. Your reaction is a reflection of your self-management.

Case study 8.5

WITH BT AGAIN

A colleague had a complaint of poor service against BT and received no joy from the local office. So annoyed was he that he decided to phone the Chairman and, somewhat to his surprise, was put through. 'Chairman's office' said the person who answered his call.

Key technique

It's a pretty safe bet that Iain Vallance, BT's chief executive, never knew of the call, but the fact that the caller heard the words 'Chairman's office' did wonders for reducing the ire that he felt as he made the call. 'Complaints department' (which it may have been) does not give the same impression. In fact, that title should never be used as the impression given is 'my goodness they must have a lot of problems if they have to have a department to deal with them'. Far better to use 'Customer care department'.

The lesson to be learned from the above is that efficiency and approach may aid the defusing of tough calls. Conversely, a lack of efficiency and even basic knowledge can only aggravate the position. A customer rang her local garage to book her car in but wanted to discuss the problems she was having with it. After a few minutes she realised that the receptionist with whom she was having the conversation knew far less about the car than she did, indeed she didn't even know how to drive, and, since the Service Manager was out, she had to ring back already annoyed at having wasted time on the first phone call.

We do need to ensure that those who are placed in the position where they have to deal with tough calls have knowledge about the subject of those calls. Ignorance will certainly not be bliss in such circumstances – indeed it can only aggravate the situation.

9
■ ■ ■

Psychological warfare

Key learning points

1 Beware – and prepare for – the person who tries to manipulate a telephone conversation.

2 Breaking a 'prepared flow' conversation is essential to avoid being forced to a pre-determined conclusion.

3 Be prepared for the 'persuasion, threat, deal' scenario – if necessary break it to gain time to think.

4 If you can fake sincerity you have it made.

5 Never lose your temper – you'll lose the discussion.

Much of the secret of dealing with tough calls is a matter of applied psychology – literally considering how best to deal with people to achieve one's own ends – and negotiation, much of which itself is concerned with psychology. What we are trying to do is, in the nicest possible way (and sometimes in anything but a nice way), to manipulate people. This sounds much worse than is intended but basically, for example, if there is a tough call and the caller is angry, the first thing we need to do is to try to defuse the anger. Innovative approaches can help – thus the call on a Sunday morning from the Chairman recounted in Case Study 7.1 went a long way to defusing the ire of the holidaymaker, whilst the sympathetic approach of the operator in Case Study 5.6 did likewise. Manipulation can sometimes go wrong, however.

134

Case study 9.1

MY BID

The director was interested in buying a business and bids had been invited. He had submitted a bid and although it had been laid down that there should be no contact other than the written bid, he phoned the other side.

'Hi there, I just wanted to check that you had received our bid.'

'Yes, we have it.'

'Everything OK?'

'Sorry, I am not sure I understand – we have the bids and will notify the appropriate party of the success of their bid and then will let everyone else know.'

'Fine, I just wanted to say that I would appreciate being given a second bite of the cherry if our bid is a bit lower than another.'

'I really cannot comment on that.'

Key technique

This puts the recipient of the bid in a very strong position, whilst to some extent destroying the credibility of the bidder. The recipient could bluff the caller's bid higher than that submitted. Similarly, since best bids were requested it indicates that the bidder has not submitted his best bid at all. The reaction from the other side since not once but twice the bidder has ignored the rules laid down (not the best bid, and making contact) could be awkward and they could refuse to consider the bid or discuss the matter further.

Putting words in the other chap's mouth
■ ■ ■

Some callers are adroit at getting their own way by manipulating the recipient. They do this by building their case logically using rhetorical questions which put words into the other party's mouth. This type of person is perhaps one of the trickiest to deal with as, unlike other tough callers, they have thought out the whole scenario as well as their reaction to alternative possibilities and responses.

Case study 9.2

RHETORICAL QUESTION DOMINATION

Following his dismissal, the former Director rang his erstwhile colleague to prepare the ground for him to promote his case for reinstatement.

'Hi, Ian, how are sales?'

'Not too bad but obviously things are tight with this recession.'

'I did say to you that you needed to keep sales buoyant, didn't I?'

'You did.' [1]

'Of course, you will be lacking my contacts now, and that won't help in the current recession. You'll have lost demand from them haven't you?'

'They have been a little slow.'

'Can't see things getting any better either – you are going to be in trouble by the end of the year unless you get sales up, aren't you?'

'It's too early to say.' [2]

'But every month that goes by with under budget sales is a drain on the cashflow as I said before didn't I?'

'That's certainly true.' [3]

'I could contact my old customers and get them to place some orders for old time's sake which would help, wouldn't it?' [4]

Key techniques

1   There is little Ian can do but agree since he has not broken the chain of questions which led to the ultimate 'statement question'. The fact that the former Director said an innumerable number of things, some of which, almost inevitably, will turn out to be correct, whilst much of the rest was irrelevant and incorrect, is overlooked.

2   Ian's former colleague has the advantage of having prepared his 'script' for the conversation in advance, has seized the initiative and is leading it towards the result he wishes to obtain. Unless Ian breaks the chain an ultimate, and, on the basis of this conversation, entirely logical, 'offer' is inevitable.

3   This rhetorical question is undeniable – facts are being delivered in a way that seeks to bolster the accuracy and prestige of the questioner.

4   With the logic built by the pre-planned conversation, the Director is put in the position of virtually having to agree, particularly since any possibility of gaining an order would be helpful.

The Baden Powell defence – 'Be prepared'

In handling this kind of person it is essential to be prepared – or if thought processes are too slow compared to the swift, prepared comment/questions, to note the suggestion and insist that you will call back later – thus providing thinking time. This alternative scenario might then take place.

Rhetorical questions – alternative scenario

'Hi, Ian, how are sales?'

'As we all anticipated they are slow, but we're reaching a lot of new contacts and hope to rectify the shortfall in the medium future.'

'I did say we need to keep sales buoyant, didn't I?'

'Well, there was nothing original in that thought – it is basic at all times, isn't it?' [1]

'But every month that passes with under budget sales is a drain on cash-flow as I warned, isn't it.'

'Again, that's stating the obvious – and to offset the effect we're endeavouring to chase every new contact, but obviously we are in competition with a number of alternative suppliers. For that reason I can't keep chatting about it – I must get on. I'll give you a ring in a couple of weeks.' [2]

Key techniques

1 This employs the rhetorical question ploy in the reverse direction.

2 Practising ending conversations can be helpful. In this case a swift resolution of the conversation before any offer is made may help. But even if not, at least it may retain or regain the initiative, forcing the other party into a reactive rather than proactive mode.

Time for thought
∎ ∎ ∎

Inherent in the above case, and indeed in many other instances where the call is at all tough is a need for time to think. It can sometimes be very difficult – even impossible – to continue a conversation whilst at the same time trying to think of all the implications and, should there be a concern regarding the creation of a precedent, what effect a decision taken now might have in the future. The devices set out below may be of use.

Stalling devices – creating thinking time

1 *'I'll have to call you back.'* This is a bit lame and it might be better to say:

2 *'I will call you back in the next few minutes,'* (which indicates a definite decision – and also an end to the present conversation).

3 *'This is an interesting point and I must give it some quiet thought – I'll ring you back shortly.'*

4 *'I'll need to refer that point to higher authority for a decision.'*

5 *'Sorry, someone distracted me – could you just run through that for me again.'*

6 *'Now that's a very interesting . . .'* (but at this point you cut the connection as if disconnected whilst you were speaking.) If you leave your phone off the hook this should give some time for thought. However, the device can really only be used once on each caller and it would be as well to ring them back as soon as possible and as soon as you have thought!

7 Catch your breath and start coughing and gasp out that you need to get a drink of water and will ring them straight back. (Note same problem and caution as in 6 above.)

8 *'Terribly sorry, I have only just popped out of a meeting to get some papers, I can't talk now – I'll ring you back in . . .'* [state time – and make sure the promise is fulfilled]. If the time is near the half hour or hour it might be believable to state that you are just about to go into a meeting but at times other than this it is less believable – as it is if it is nearly lunch time.

9 *'Sorry, I've just started an interview, I can't break off now – I'll ring you back as soon as I am free.'*

10 *'Sorry, I'm in the middle of a rush job for the Chairman and I really cannot stop now – will ring you back . . .'*

11 Arrange a code with your secretary so that (s)he can break into the conversation with an 'urgent request' for you to go somewhere or see someone.

12 *'Sorry, the Chairman has just walked into the office – I'll call you back.'*

The underlying point of most of these is that they are lies to gain time and it could be argued that the best approach might be to tell the truth: *'Sorry, that raises a number of points which I want to consider carefully and quietly – I'll have to get back to you'.*

Making a deal
∎ ∎ ∎

The rhetorical questioning can be carried a stage further by a persistent caller whereby (s)he embarks on a process of three structured phases and calls. Of course, the respondent does not realise until the completion of the last call that they have been manipulated by the caller. Such callers have done all their thinking previously and part of the process requires that the respondent does not have time, and does not gain time by using one of the above suggested devices to break the process and stall the movement towards the caller's desired result.

In this sequence, the caller first raises a question indicating his or her preparedness to find a suitable and reasonable solution, even if it is not their own desired result. After a reasonable response or compromise has been indicated, the attitude of the caller then hardens with inference of threats if that desired result is not agreed. Finally, the caller moves to the third stage where a deal is suggested.

Case study 9.3

1 PERSUASION, 2 THREAT, 3 DEAL

The first part of this structured trap uses an encounter such as is set out in Case Study 9.2 above, ie an offer, seemingly without strings, to try and assist sales demand through using personal contacts. Thus the conversation (first alternative) could have ended

1 Persuasion

'What I can do is to speak to a few of my old contacts and get them to place orders, which will help won't it?'

'It would.'

'I'll tell you what I'll do – no hard feelings for what has gone before, that's just business, not personal. I'll make a few phone calls to all my old contacts and tell them that there are no differences between us and they would be doing themselves a favour by placing their orders as before, that's in everyone's interests isn't it?' [1]

2 Threat
One or two days after the above conversation, the former Director telephones Ian again.

'Ian, I've just been with my solicitor and he says that there is a cast iron case against the company for unfair dismissal, and I should take action immediately, in order to protect my position, though that's not in anyone's interest is it?'

'Not really – I thought we had agreed a compromise.'

'So did I, but he feels that to protect my interests I should take action immediately for the maximum claimable. Obviously the compensation awarded could hit the company hard when things are tough, but since I am paying him for his advice, I have to listen to what he says don't I?'

'I suppose you do.' [2]

3 Deal
Again a couple of days are left before the caller calls Ian again.

'Ian, I've spoken to some of my contacts and I am sure that I can put together a number of orders which will help the order book now and cash flow next month.'

'Oh great.'

'I've also had another chat with my solicitor who is adamant that there is a strong case.'

'Oh yes.'

'Mind you, it seems a bit pointless for us to argue in a tribunal when we could make the company profitable with my contacts doesn't it?'

'I suppose so.'

'What did cross my mind was for me to drop the action.'

'That would be good news.'

'Yes, it would save aggro all round. Mind you, I think I should get some-thing out of it. I'd suggest in return you appoint me on a consultancy basis for, say, six months, to try and generate some sales during the present slump. If you pay me on commission it won't even cost you a thing.' [3]

Key techniques

1 On the face of it, this does seem to help everyone, but of course the point of such an offer is to give the former director an edge which can be exploited from a different angle later.

2 Once again the rhetorical question is being used to force the apparently unquestionable progress to the position required. What must not be overlooked here of course, is that the whole thing may be a bluff. The solicitor may not have indicated such advice or even have been consulted at all, yet the underlying threat has been made. To counter this Ian would need to bluff in return responding to the advice that his former colleague had consulted a solicitor with the retort 'Oh really – we've also taken advice and our people think there's no case to answer.' rather than referring to the compromise already 'agreed', and stating 'you must take what action you feel correct'.

3 This provides the crunch and given the way Ian answered the two prongs on which the deal rests, it may be difficult for him to find suitable words with which to extricate himself.

141

This is the problem with submitting to the power of the phone. Because it is there on our desk it can interrupt every-thing and because the voice is in our ear and brain it can demand an answer. Because we answer the call and become involved in a conversation, if we are not firm and in control, we can become conditioned to the continuation of the matter and are virtually forced to make a decision. Despite this con-ditioning effect it is very often advisable to break the chain and insist that time is taken to consider what may require proper consideration rather than making a decision on the spur of the moment simply because we have been so conditioned. If Ian is aware of this conditioning effect he may be able to either interrupt the flow and take a break or turn the tables with statements of his own.

DEAL – ALTERNATIVE SCENARIO

'Ian, I've spoken to some of my contacts and I am sure that I can put together a number of orders which will help the order book now and cash flow next month and in the following months.'

'That's fine – but we do need firm orders confirmed in writing via one of the representatives, so if you drop me a line with the details I'll pass them on to the appropriate representative. We'll pay you an introduction fee on any orders generated of course.'

'I've also had another chat with my solicitor who is adamant that there is a strong case.'

'As I said before – our advice is different, but you must take such action as you think fit.'

'It seems a bit pointless for us to argue in a tribunal when we could make the company profitable with my contacts doesn't it?'

'I can see that, but of course the two items are entirely separate – we can both benefit from any orders you can generate. If you take legal action, which of course may be costly for you, we will have to sort that out at the appropriate time and place. I don't see that the one affects the other in any way.'

Firmly separating the two aspects of the 'would-be' deal in this way negates the former Director's progress to his desired result, and weakens his case for compensation!

Assertiveness

■ ■ ■

The essential characteristic of the caller in Case Studies 9.2 and 9.3 is one of assertiveness bordering on the aggressive. But two can play at that game and those forced to deal with tough calls and tricky customers like Ian's former colleague may need to develop assertiveness of their own. This can be somewhat difficult for those not normally assertive and particularly for the diffident. It may also be difficult to distinguish between aggression and assertiveness. The aggressive person (who wants to throw their weight around and, above all, to be noticed) attempts to gain their own way virtually by steamrollering all opposition – no-one is allowed views of their own or to hold a contrary opinion – everything must be sublimated to their views. They may hear what is being said but will rarely listen and very seldom compromise – to such a person it's all or nothing. The assertive person sees things somewhat differently.

Principles of assertiveness

The assertive person needs to say to themselves (and if pushed may actually state to an aggressive person with whom they are interfacing or having a tough call):

143

'I have the right
- *to put my views forward and have them listened to by you,*
- *to ask you for information and explanation and be answered,*
- *to disagree with your views,*
- *to take time out to consider where we are (see 'stalling devices' page 138),*
- *to change my views.*

Note that changing one's mind should not be viewed as a weakness. It is really a strength which shows that you have listened to others and taken note of what they have to say – it may also soften their stance and enable you to gain concessions.

In *Thinking on Your Feet in Negotiation* Jane Hodgson refers to research conducted by the Huthwaite Group who found that those who explained the reasons for not agreeing with others before indicating that they could not agree were the more successful negotiators. What this is saying is that plain good manners works. In taking a little time to explain one's viewpoint or rationale first, one's opponents are being treated as respected equals. Closing off the relationship with an unexplained negative (which is the action of the aggressive person) is equivalent to dismissing the opponents and their views as an irrelevance.

Concessions may be won in the first instance as some kind of rapport still exists. It is, however, extremely unlikely that the reaction of one's opponents in the alternative scenario will be anything other than irritation – there will certainly be no rapport between the parties and is unlikely to be any agreed solution to a tough call.

Sincere lying
■ ■ ■

The guidance given to the young salesman is perhaps appropriate – *'Son, if you can fake sincerity then you have got it made.'* Alright, so faked sincerity is a contradiction in terms – an oxymoron – and some will regard it as being hypocritical. Nevertheless, if you can give to the caller the impression that you are genuinely concerned to find a solution to their problem and appreciate all the difficulties it may be causing (like the operator in Case Study 5.6) then most callers will tend to respond to that sincerity and it will help defuse the situation. Similarly I cannot believe that a few white lies (for example 'the Chairman was very concerned about your query and has asked me to ring you' when the nearest the Chairman got to the call was that it was put through to one of several employees put there for that very purpose – as presumably was the situation in Case Study 8.5) are not acceptable provided they defuse the aggravation and move the problem on to a solution which may not be ideal but is at least acceptable.

Temper
■ ■ ■

The problems with temper are that:

144

1 it tends to generate temper although it must also be realised that a person dealing calmly with a person who has lost their temper may actually further aggravate the one seized by temper by their very calmness;

2 it often creates a frustration in the one so seized since they are unable to express themselves as they wish (indeed this can often be the cause of the temper as well as one of its effects);

3 things are said which are not meant – exaggerations are used in order to try and make the case stronger (in fact this can often have the opposite effect since if a row develops exaggerations can be held up and exposed as being false. Since they are false this can question and undermine the rest of the case which might otherwise be strong);

4 it may become difficult to understand the real point of the call;

5 the desired result is completely forgotten or sublimated or overtaken by a substituted result – telling the respondent what you think of them! This alternative result may be very understandable and may also enable the caller to let off steam but it will not necessarily enable them to move to what they wanted in that control and the advantage, provided they can keep calm, is immediately handed to the other side.

145

Case study 9.4

NOT WHAT SHE WANTED – BUT SHE MAY FEEL BETTER

The client had departed on her holiday leaving the placement agency to make arrangements for a replacement au pair that she had selected to travel to the UK on the client's return. During the time the client was on holiday, both a former au pair and a neighbour contacted the agency to lodge complaints about the client. The agency could hardly ignore the complaints and decided the only thing to do was to advise the replacement au pair that complaints had been lodged, although it could not check their accuracy, and leave it to her to decide whether to withdraw or not. She decided to withdraw and the agency wrote to the client explaining this and returning the whole of their fee, so that the client would be free and in funds to contact other agencies. In this they went beyond the terms the client had accepted which allowed them to retain part of the fee. On her return the client was furious about the whole situation and in a state of considerable temper phoned the agency. They tried to explain the situation calmly but the client insisted on talking over their words each time and asking rhetorical questions on which the agency refused to be drawn, simply repeating that in the circumstances they felt it would be better if she used another agency. [1] & [2]

'But you are saying you believe these people who have complained.'

'No, we are not – we cannot know – we . . .'

'Rubbish, you are believing them without asking me for my view.'

'That is not true. We had to advise . . .'[3]

'I find your comments insulting and patronising.'

'I'm sorry but I am trying to explain our . . .'

'You're explaining nothing, you are all hot air – you obviously believe the lies these people have concocted rather than believing me.'

'We cannot make such a judgement and we do not wish to . . .'[4]

'That's just ****, you've offered me no ******* explanation.'

'I'm sorry I have been trying but please understand that it is difficult to explain if I can't finish explaining our points.'

'Don't be so ****** rude.' (Conversation terminated by client slamming down the phone.) [5]

Key techniques

1 It seemed that the client was deliberately trying to provoke the agency into some kind of heated response which presumably would have provided a peg on which she could then hang her frustration at the developments, and provide her with an edge for future action.

2 As we saw earlier, using rhetorical questions is a device which enables the devious to trap the unwary into statements or commitments which may be somewhat at variance to those they would make willingly, or when not under pressure.

3 The agency representative constantly tried to bring the conversation back to the facts and avoided being drawn into commenting or rebutting the client's contentions – insulting and often untrue though these were. Keeping calm can be very difficult in such situations but there is no alternative – cool professionalism is the only defence.

4 To cover the agency's position a letter was sent outlining its position and regretting that the conversation had been terminated in such an abrupt manner – quoting the actual words used by the client. The desired result as far as the agency was concerned was to extricate itself from a 'no-win' situation, and by recording aspects of the encounter in writing, which of course hardly reflected well on the client, to avoid any possibility of subsequent action.

5 The desired result from the client's viewpoint, apart from venting her extreme anger and frustration, is difficult to visualise. Certainly being aggressive was hardly likely to encourage the agency to retain her as a client – much the reverse. Indeed, the display of anger, frustration and foul language rather supported the complaints lodged, whilst the repetition of insults made against the agency were hardly likely to endear her to them. 'Lose your temper – lose the argument' was very evident here.

Power of silence
■ ■ ■

It should not be overlooked of course that simply keeping quiet in such circumstances may actually win the day though not necessarily win the argument. After all, in Case Study 9.4 if the agency had not commented, ultimately the caller would have run out of steam and the agency might have been able to put its own points across in the call rather than in the letter. Many people have a problem with silence and rush to fill it. The classic scenario is the television interview where the subject is being grilled. If instead of arguing and even, as in some celebrated instances, trying to walk out on the interview albeit a device rendered impossible because of a voice mike connected to their clothing, they had simply said 'no comment' the interview would need to be brought to an end as silence does not make good viewing – confrontation means peak viewing figures.

Case study 9.5

COSTLY SILENCE

The agent had been instructed to get as much for the letting as possible and had one potential tenant who was very interested in the property and had put in an offer. The landlord had told the agent that he would accept the figure put forward by the tenant.

The agent rang the tenant and said that he had been chatting about the offer to the landlord. He then paused.

The tenant, after a few seconds, was tempted by the silence and said that he had been thinking things over and would be prepared to slightly increase his offer. The agent simply said 'Mmmm' and kept quiet. The tenant then increased his offer to above the figure stated by the landlord to be acceptable.

Key technique

Sometimes simply waiting can put considerable pressure on the other side.

This is not meant to suggest that we should respond to a genuine and concerned caller with a silence which may be understandably taken as insulting, but that if our caller is rude, aggressive or abusive (or indeed all three) then it may be better to keep quiet and let them run themselves out of steam. Any enquiry as to why they have not received a response can be met with a polite 'I thought it might be helpful if I allowed you to get everything off your chest first and then checked a few details. It is easier to discover the facts when we deal with things calmly.' If this is said in an entirely neutral voice it should not upset most people whilst if it is said very quietly it will force the person to stop shouting and to listen which may itself give them an opportunity to regain some self-control. Keeping your voice in a low key and talking softly will sustain the pressure on the other party to concentrate on what you are saying and may again allow temper to subside. Conversely a rising pitch in a voice indicates a loss of control. At least the one consolation when dealing with temper loss is that the person is at the other end of the phone line and cannot punch you on the nose.

149

10

. . .

Cold calling
– in the blue corner

Key learning points

1 Exponents of cold calling programmes need to train those employed to make such calls and provide adequate pre-call preparation. Data about the subject are essential.

2 We need to contrive or determine 'hooks' to try to gain a positive response from the target respondent.

3 Cold callers need to prepare carefully, with due regard for the susceptibilities of the respondents and never assume or take anything for granted.

4 Finding out personal details about the target, trying to gain personal contact, and having an original 'hook' may gain a greater chance of success.

Alternative scenarios

■ ■ ■

Imagine you are watching television and in the middle of one of your favourite programmes comes the commercial break. Unless the programme is particularly gripping, the intervention of the two minutes break for advertising is normally accepted for what it is, and little annoyance is created. Indeed, in some instances, it may be welcomed particularly if included in the break is one of our favourite advertisements which uses a storyline to promote the product or an alternative which particularly appeals to our sense of humour, and so on. Now say you change channels to BBC where there are no commercial breaks but as one programme ends the phone lying by your chair rings. You answer it and a voice tells you that their double-glazing team is in your 'area' and can provide a good deal for the replacement of your windows and doors. Such an interruption, is, if my research can be relied upon, likely to cause considerable annoyance and frustration to the majority of people.

Neither 'break' interrupted the story – in one everything stopped for the adverts, whilst in the other the programmes were changing, so in neither case did we lose anything. Yet both advert and call are essentially cold sells.

■ In neither case are the supplier and the customer linked other than by a channel of telecommunication.

■ Both use a scattergun approach, ie if you make your product known to enough people some will buy, hopefully enough to make it worth your while advertising the product in the first place.

■ In neither case does the advertiser know whether or not the customer requires the product – part of the purpose of both is to create demand and also satisfy it.

■ In neither case is the advertiser responding to an enquiry from the consumer.

Given all these similarities why is it that we can be so relatively relaxed about the commercial breaks, to which we are subjected roughly every 15 minutes on a repeating basis, and object so much to the telephoning double-glazing (and the alternatives including timeshare selling, subscription services, health care, utilities cost-saving and directories) salesperson? Perhaps if we can identify our objections it may help both the cold calling salesperson to become more effective as well as helping those who object to the device to become more adept at terminating the call swiftly.

Commercial breaks *versus* cold calling

1 When we turn on the television we 'invite' into our homes both the product of the programme makers as well as the means by which those programmes are funded – the advertisers.

153

As far as the telephone cold call we give no such invite other than a very indirect one by allowing our number to be listed in the directory. The simple answer to avoid cold calling on a personal basis is to withdraw our number from the directory but this is not feasible for businesses.

2 Because the television has an off-switch we therefore have control.

Other than unplugging the phone which may be inconvenient for other callers we have no control over our callers.

3 Many advertisements are mini-programmes in their own right and have an appeal – in short they continue the entertainment we seek (indeed part of a widespread complaint is that often the creativity displayed in the adverts is far higher than that displayed in the programmes!).

A cold call telephone call normally lacks interest and any entertainment value whatsoever.

4 We can appreciate the creativity in the advert as well as the message it is trying to convey.

Most telephone selling calls are conducted by low skill callers with little knowledge, creativity, etc. – their interest is not in selling the product but in gaining a possible contact for which they will be paid.

5 The advertiser has a direct interest in trying to create demand in the viewer and endeavours to appeal to them.

Often the caller has little direct interest in the person being called other than as 'the next name on the list which I'm being paid to go through'.

6 We are required to provide no input to the television advertisement – other than to watch it.

We have to respond to the telephone caller – often knowing that every one of our responses has the corresponding answer on the caller's list so the call can be protracted.

7 Television advertisements are extremely expensive to produce so the advertiser's hidden message is 'this is costly but it's worth it to try and win you, the consumer, as a customer'.

Telephoning is relatively cheap so no great value is being granted by the caller to the person answering the phone. This is particularly so when the respondent has already replaced all their windows and doors so it is obvious that the caller has no knowledge whatever of their requirements.

8 Few advertisements last where the message insults the intelligence of the viewer.

Some cold calling, particularly for products such as timeshares insult the intelligence of the recipient – offering gifts of considerable value without apparent cost. To misquote Margaret Thatcher 'there is no such thing as a free gift'.

The way forward?

■ ■ ■

To those required to cold call the answer perhaps could be said to lie in trying to adopt the approach highlighted by the differences identified in the list above. We need our cold call to

- try to minimise any inconvenience,

- contain an interest which does not insult the intelligence,

- contain a degree of creativity which entices,

- be conducted by someone who understands what they are doing and appreciates the low regard with which many cold calling operations are held and attempts to compensate for this.

155

Case study 10.1

A 'GOOD' EXAMPLE?

'Please could I speak to the person who would deal with your business rates.' [1]

'That's me.'

'We are a company of rates consultants with an excellent record in obtaining massive reductions and reassessments.' [2]

'Oh yes.'

'Our representative is in your area tomorrow and would like to make an appointment to see the person who deals with your rates.' [3]

'And what's the idea?'

'We will carry out a survey of the rates you are paying and show you how to save at least 10 per cent, but before doing so we do need an up front fee of £250 which will be more than covered by the savings we can show you.'

'I'm not interested in any service where I have to pay in advance.' [4]

'We only insist on that because we have experienced problems with bad debts before and as a small organisation can be badly hit when people do not pay their bills.' [5]

The encounter on which this is based was recounted by Syd Rawcliffe in the *Administrator*. Having turned down the invitation his phone rang again later with the same opening spiel, and again, and again. In all, he was contacted by the same woman ringing on behalf of the same organisation no less than five times in a single day. [6, 7 & 8]

Key techniques

1 The opening line is a dead giveaway that it is a cold caller – they do not know who they wish to speak to and are fishing for a contact

Requirement: Find out who you wish to speak to. It is relatively easy to ring most organisations and say 'I have something to send to the person dealing with rates – but I want to address it to him or her personally – could you tell me their name and position'. With this information the cold caller can at least make progress from the main switchboard to the office of the target. The other advantage, should the follow up call actually get through to the target, is that the cold caller can say 'Good morning Mr Jones, its Peter Frost of Rate-U-Like here' creating at least some link between the parties. It may also create an impression that the caller may be someone the executive has met somewhere – they may even have asked them to call . . . so the stage is set (see more detailed advice on this point later).

2 Yes and so am I. Anyone can claim this and in Syd's encounter when he eventually saw the representative and asked for names of such referees the information 'wasn't available'. Once again this insults the intelligence of the respondent.

Solutions

a Get such recommendations – better still get a recommendation from a previously satisfied client addressed to the prospective client, introducing the service. Of course if the old client is known to the new client that link should at least ensure there is an opening gambit. In the absence of a link it might help if the recommendations were sent ahead.

b If recommendations are sent ahead they need to be personally addressed to the target. The follow up (also personally addressed) can then refer to the hard evidence already submitted. The ice has been broken by the written contact which may also help the subsequent verbal discussion.

3 This shows an initial lack of concentration whilst the second part of the sentence may be seen as the lie it probably is. The respondent has already stated that he deals with the rates, so implying that there is a lack of knowledge of this point indicates poor administration and efficiency which is hardly a good indication of the service that may be expected should the organisation be retained to carry out the work.

The suggestion that someone will be 'in your area' is so corny as to be deserving of being ignored as an almost certain lie by most respondents.

Solutions

a When the respondent stated that he dealt with the rates, the immediate follow up question should have been – 'could I possibly have your name, sir' which should then have been written by the caller in large letters on the pad next to the telephone number being called and his name should have been used during the conversation to try and build a rapport.

b It might be more advisable to suggest that the caller attempts to make an appointment 'at a time convenient to you, sir' rather than attempting to con the respondent who, if they have been in business any length of time, have heard such a spiel many times before.

c Avoid treating respondents as if they have no intelligence. Such is the growth in the reliance on cold calling in this way that most businesses receive such calls weekly. The common hidden message that 'we can run your business more cost-effectively than you' is a hook which may be correct but needs to be tempered with tact.

4 I am sure practically every business has experienced bad debts at
& some time in their existence. The fact that the caller has had such
5 problems is their problem and nothing to do with a prospective client. Why should they be expected to fund the caller's mistakes or misfortune?

Solutions

a Such a service if it has faith in its ability should really be prepared to deal on the basis of a split of the savings – in other words 'putting its money where its mouth is'.

b In addition, in stating the problem at this early stage in the encounter the organisation is providing all the wrong signals. Few, if any, businessmen or women with any experience will view this as anything other than pretty sharp practice.

6 This is a really great advert for the efficiency of the organisation.
& Pretty obviously the caller is someone who, given inadequate brief-
7 ing regarding making such a call, inadequate training in handling people and obviously hasn't even read this book, has been handed some numbers and told to 'try and get me an interview with some-one on this list'. Indeed, the respondent may have more experience in handling such calls than the caller, and might even be tempted to offer a service showing how they could cut the cost of their tele-phone bill by proper control of the placing of such calls! Ensuring those already called are crossed off the list or, only if successful, passed on to the next stage would help both sides immeasurably.

Solutions

a Proper product and service training so that the caller knows what is on offer.

b Adequate training in how to make and progress the call with due regard for the susceptibilities of the respondent (who, if they were not annoyed by the first or second calls, will be getting pretty annoyed by the fifth interruption).

c A proper system for making such calls so that each has a slip with the target's name plus as much information about their organisation as possible so that the caller can speak from some experience of their set-up. Where a call is successful, the slip should be moved to a 'follow up' file with any additional information added to it. Where the call is unsuccessful, it should be moved to a 'failed' file but before doing so the number should be deleted from all lists so that there are no further wasted calls. (Of course it may be required to move it to a 'try again in six months' file rather than writing off as a complete loss.)

8 The caller would not be human if, being paid on the basis of a commission on successful calls, as most people making these calls are, his or her disappointment at receiving another 'no sale' message did not colour the way in which they deal with the calls.

Each call tends to become a repetitive spiel with less and less commitment and enthusiasm.

Solution

Encourage the caller to write their own script and determine their own way of doing things subject to proper (and not exaggerated) claims regarding the product/service. Monitor how each call is handled and suggest ways of improving the patter.

Solutions

∎ ∎ ∎

Two of the most important aspects of cold calling highlighted as part of the commentary on Case Study 10.1 are

- speaking to the right person and
- having the right script

and it is apposite to concentrate on these two items.

Speaking to the right person

Far too many cold callers assume that they can make contact with the person who has authority to give them what they want (eg an order, an appointment, etc.) simply by asking the telephonist to put them through to their target. However, any manager who is plagued by cold callers (for example, buyers, company secretaries, directors) can avoid this simply by instructing the telephonist not to put such calls through. The telephonist can be instructed to reply:

'I am sorry, the only way you can contact Mr/Ms Bloggs is by writing in to us' or by stating

'We do not conduct business over the phone. Please attend at [time] when all representatives are seen.'

However, this can be circumvented fairly easily – all the cold caller needs to do is to discover the name of the person they need to speak to and a little ingenuity will do this for them.

A sop for Cerebus

Greek mythology has it that Cerebus was a massive three-headed dog that guarded Hades (the Underworld). Aeneas, a Trojan prince, whose exploits are recounted in Virgil's *Aeneid*, needed to get past Cerebus and into Hades, and to do so, soaked a piece of bread in honey and a soporific and threw it to the dog. Cerebus ate it and went to sleep allowing Aeneas to slip past.

Getting your target's name

'Cerebus – the first head'

1 Ring the switchboard and state

'I've got to send a sample to your [buyer, company secretary, chief executive, etc.] but I don't have his full name.'

This implies that you are responding to a request from the target and that he knows you. Of course this device may fall flat if the target is a woman, although the quick-witted in reply to

'Our [buyer] is a lady'

might be able to recover with

'I do beg her pardon – you are quite right – it's my bad writing. I thought I put Mr but I can see now I wrote Ms.'

The original contact line can be further extended and when the telephonist replies

'You mean Mr(Ms) Jones' you reply

'Oh I've been given his(her) surname but I wanted to personalise it by using his(her) first name' (remember to avoid the use of the word 'Christian' in case (s)he is not).

Conversely, if the telephonist says

'Oh you mean Bert' you could reply

'I know it's Bert – I just need to know his surname.'

2 Ring the target organisation and ask to be put through to the Accounts department as you have a query on an invoice. Often such a call will be put through without question. When you are put through you state

'Oh, I think I've been put through to the wrong extension. I wanted to speak to your buyer – now what's his name – I've got it somewhere here . . .' (rustling papers).

Once again the inference is that you are known to the organisation in general and the buyer in particular. The poor respondent in Accounts will be only too glad to provide the name and may even offer to put you through! It is unlikely if this respondent will have the skill of the telephonist in filtering out such unwanted calls. (Of course, if they say they will put you back to the telephonist it might be wise to break the connection.)

3 When the telephonist answers your cold call – state

'sorry – I didn't catch that'.

The telephonist will almost certainly repeat the name of the organisation and you reply

'Yes, I know, but I thought I was taking a call from you – I think someone in your buying department – was it Mr . . . no, sorry, I can't find the note I made of his name – who do you have in that department who could have called me?'

Again the inference is that you are known to the organisation and the buyer's name or someone in that department may be forthcoming.

4 Obtain a copy of the accounts of the organisation which lists all the names of the directors (if you can't be bothered to check the file kept at Companies House, ring the company and ask them to send you a copy). Once you have that you have a choice of directors' names you could ask for – and quoting both forename and surname will tend to get you put through to their office at least, since again the inference is that you are known to them. A variation can be to say to the receptionist,

'I was speaking to your [production, personnel, managing] director a short time ago and he suggested I give your [buyer, production manager, retail controller] a ring but I have mislaid the note I took at the time with his name and extension.'

Warning: don't say 'I met' or be too specific about when you spoke as this can fall flat if the managing director, for example, has been on a sabbatical for a year or with the USA parent company for two months.

The secret is bluff – and a few white lies. The reward is the name of the person you need to speak to.

All that these devices result in is getting the target's name for the cold caller. However, armed with this, the cold caller can usually make progress to the office of the target where he will encounter the second head.

162 *Getting through to the target*

'Cerebus – the second head'

In most companies of any size the target will have a secretary or personal assistant who will almost certainly be primed to fend off unwanted callers as was the telephonist. Having gained the name of the target however, the cold caller can infer that he is known to the target and thus, being known, that the defences can be relaxed for him.

1   *'Hallo, this is Fred Jones of XYZ, is Bert Robinson free for a few moments?'*

   Again, the tone is familiar and the inference is that Fred is known to Bert and that Bert will be happy to spare him a few moments on the phone. There is an underlying additional inference that Bert may have even asked Fred to phone him.

2   *'Hallo, this is Fred Jones, I know Bert Robinson must be up to his ears in it at the moment, but I wonder if I could have a quick word with him about our widget that he wants to see.'*

   The inference here once again is of familiarity with the added seductive point for the guardian that the call is likely to be a quick one. The bluff *'that he wants to see'* can be argued if challenged as *'Well, I was certain he would want to see it once he knew what it could do'* though this may be stretching things somewhat.

3 Even more progress can be made if, using similar devices to those set out above, you find out the secretary's own name.

'Hallo Jo, I don't think we've met – this is Fred Jones of XYZ, has Bert got a few moments free?'

This is applied psychology – ie person manipulation. If the secretary is used to being Mr, Mrs or Miss Anonymous and, as such, is often virtually ignored by callers (both in the flesh and on the phone) (s)he may respond warmly to being addressed by name and it may distract him or her from keeping up their normal defences. The very familiarity sets a scene from which it may be difficult to generate the usual frosty response.

163

4 Claiming to have met the target may also infer a personal request/contact which can overcome hostility.

'Hallo Jo, Fred Jones of XYZ here. I met your Mr Robinson at a conference and he found a number of developments interesting so we're trying to fix up a time to get together.'
This goes past the need to bother Bert at this moment – all we need to do is arrange a suitable time for the caller to visit.

5 The inference that the cold caller has been asked to call can be further strengthened by using the device that a third party, known to the target, suggested the call was made. This is a high risk bluff which entails using a name of a director or similar (obtained from the Annual Report as above or from some other source) and inferring that the cold caller is complying with *their* request.

'Oh hallo, this is Fred Jones of XYZ, I think it was your [managing director) Alf Smith who suggested that I give Bert Robinson a ring to fix up an appointment to review our latest widgets.'

If the bluff is called the conditional aspect of this comment can be explained away –

'Oh perhaps I've got my notes mixed up, we've had a minor fire here and things are a bit confused'.

Ideally, in the instances of both scenarios 4 and 5, this might lead to the secretary fixing up an appointment but at least it should get you past the secretary and on to meet the last of Cerebus' three heads.

There is nothing particularly clever or even original about the devices suggested above. The secret is that in giving attention to preparatory work progress should, in many cases, have been made well past the switchboard. Indeed, if information on the company has been obtained in advance, knowledge of its business, trading record and so on may well stand the cold caller in good stead. There needs to be a warning sounded however – liars have got to have good memories, and the way in which any link to the target was induced should be noted in case of later questions.

Originality

The main problem with cold calling is that most callers lack originality and the call itself is a dreary repetition of standard phrases. Organisations adopting this method of selling need to determine their Unique Selling Proposition (USP) and if they haven't got one then they need to find one and promote it rather than simply trying to promote their product. It is unlikely that a USP can rely solely on price – basically since it will probably not be believed, and, besides it is hardly original nor unique anyway. We need to determine what it is that makes our product unique and whether we can use this to entice people to give it further consideration, using the telephone as a means of doing so. If the answer is that we have not got such a factor then telephone selling is probably not the correct approach.

The sops to tempt Cerebus to buy

'Cerebus – the third head'

Cold callers need to accept that they are not trying to sell a product but trying to convince the respondent that he or she is buying a solution. There needs to be a 'hook' that will entice a positive response. If we think of the commercial break again, many adverts sell their products using

- humour
- a perception of value
- convenience (saving time)

whilst some 'tease' by displaying hints or part messages which our brain retains (even puzzles about) until we can put the whole message together or are told the whole message. This is somewhat easier to do visually and we may determine that cold cold-calling is out and what we need to do is to soften the respondents up first with a visual 'hook'. If so, it needs to be impressive and eye-catching and above all must convey a simple message which can be used in the subsequent call.

'Have a laugh with us'

165

Original humour may assist the caller to gain at least the right to an audience.

Case study 10.2

WINNING THE LOTTERY

A business gifts company sent out a key-ring with a board containing 49 holes into which six tiny ball bearings could be shaken in order to determine a suggested set of 'winning' numbers for a National Lottery entry. Subsequently, a representative rang.

'This is Bob from Business Gifts – I just rang to see if you won the Lottery last week using our number selector key-ring?'

'No.'

'So you haven't given up work yet then – in that case would you be interested in buying a few key-rings or some other novel ideas we've come up with?'

Key technique

Humour and a topical high profile item are being used to break the ice – which has already been broken to some extent by sending something a little unusual as a 'hook' or teaser.

A variation could be to send a written follow-up after the following Lottery draw 'sorry to see you were not amongst the winners – but we still have some prizes you might like to win.'

Note: The ultimate non-teaser is the call which refers to something which has not been sent at all. This hook without a hook can be very irritating particularly as sometimes the caller can almost give the impression that the respondent is pretending not to have received the item. One begins to wonder in such a situation who is trying to sell to whom!

'We'll oversee the change'

We might determine that one way in which we could sell our (for example) health insurance cover is by stressing that all the administration regarding the change will be handled by us. It should not be overlooked that busy people may be unwilling to add to their load and agreeing to change suppliers even for a price reduction, may not be attractive when they consider the amount of work they are going to have to undertake to make the change. Offering a service that takes this chore off their hands might be attractive but entails a commitment.

Case study 10.3

HEALTHY SIGNS

'Hallo Miss Robinson, I appreciate your time is limited but I think I have a way of saving you some time and also saving your organisation some money.'

'Oh, what's that?'

'Here at Healthy Options we've devised a new way of covering your executives' health needs and the good news is that we will do all the administration to cope with the change. All you have to do is okay our proposal and we'll come in and do all the rest of the paperwork for you. And once it's all done you'll find that your firm will have saved around 20 per cent of its annual health insurance costs.'

Key technique

This is an upbeat approach and might be best preceded by a mail shot showing how the savings are effected and quoting previously satisfied customers so that the target can verify the claims.

'We're original'

Originality is perhaps the rarest of qualities – in this it is both a challenge and an opportunity. If we can capture some originality and market this, since it is rare, we may find our attempts are well received since the target audience can respond to the unfamiliar stimuli.

Case study 10.4
TASTY MORSEL

A business information publisher ordered ten times as many of the first chapter of a new business guide as they needed for the finished book and used the chapter as a mail shot to tempt recipients to buy the rest of the guide.

'Hallo Mr Spencer, this is Gill from Business Information. We sent you part of our new business guide to property last week and I wondered if you'd had a chance to read it yet?'[1]

'Yes I did skip through it.'

'We've had a very good response to the sample. Most people I've spoken to seem to feel that it fits the bill very well. The whole guide is available and if you would like it I can send it to you on a seven days' free approval basis. That will give you some time to skip [2] through the rest and see if it meets the needs of your organisation. If it does and you want to keep it we'll simply invoice you at the end of the month.'

167

Key techniques

1 Nothing is assumed. If Mr Spencer is busy then he may not like it being assumed that he has time to look through a guide.

2 Using a word that the respondent has used may add to the rapport which the caller is trying to build. However, this may be a little dangerous as it may be taken as sarcasm.

Of course, this works somewhat better with fiction than with business books but it can aid effectiveness. It's not a bad spur to encourage authors to get going on their theme rather than spending too much time on introductions!

11

. . .

Cold calling
– in the red corner

Key learning points

1 To fend off unwanted cold (and other) calls develop the continuous closing sentence which does not allow interruption and enables you to reach a 'goodbye' without leaving the caller a 'peg' on which to hang another sentence.

2 Determining which of the several types of cold callers is calling can focus the mind on the best response with which to close the call.

3 It is essential to be firm to close down cold and unwanted calls.

4 Preparing and practising antidotes to cold calling will aid the abbreviation and termination of such calls.

Erecting the defences
■ ■ ■

Chapter Ten concentrated on ways in which those faced with the task of making cold calls might make their task more easy and become more effective. Those charged with the task of making cold calls tend to be a small but possibly vociferous minority. Most readers, however, may feel that they would prefer to be coached in effective means of closing down such encounters before the caller has time to get well into the script that many have available in front of them or even off by heart.

Case study 11.1
NOT SO HEALTHY

'Hallo, this is Jackie from Healthy Options. I'm calling to see if you have any health cover.'

'Yes, we have.'

'Then let me tell you about our alternative.'

Key technique

In terms of trying to fend off unwanted calls this has failed since Jackie has now got her foot figuratively in the door and can begin to run through the rest of the script.

'Hallo, this is Jackie from Healthy Options. Could I speak to a partner?' [1]

'Speaking.'

'I'm calling to see if you have any health cover.'

'Yes, we have and we're perfectly happy with it and don't wish to change – thank you for your call.'[2]

Key techniques

1 This telegraphs to the respondent that this is a cold call – thus allowing them to be prepared – remember that it usually takes around 10 seconds for the respondent to focus on the caller and what they want. This few seconds preparation allows them to have the answer to the next questions ready and waiting.

2 Conversation closed off.

Not simply answering Jackie's question but moving past it to make a statement of one's own wrests the initiative from the caller.

Effectively two messages have been conveyed to Jackie:

■ firstly the spoken message is that this organisation does not wish to contemplate a change, and

■ secondly the unspoken message is that 'I have rumbled the fact that this is a cold call and I do not wish to discuss this, and want to get on with the work you have interrupted'.

If Jackie tries to push it further she risks aggravating the respondent which is hardly the best way to win friends. Her best response will be a positive one:

'Okay sorry to have bothered you – thanks for your time – you don't mind if we contact you in a few months' time to see if the position has changed, do you?'

This will almost certainly bring forth the answer:

'No, that's fine – goodbye.'

since in that way without being rude the respondent can close off the whole encounter, although the actual closure has only been deferred.

In Case Study 11.1 the encounter was closed down almost completely. If the initial response which grasps control from the caller is missed then an alternative may be necessary. Ironically, two weeks later the same company called the same respondent and asked the same question. Hardly surprisingly, Jackie received the same reply as she did when she rang again after a further two weeks.

She may not have been aware she had already spoken to the partner twice before – but he was. The result of such poor administration is of course merely to demonstrate to the respondent that they made the right decision. After all, if the callers are as inefficient with their health care as they are with their cold calling who is likely to be attracted to them?

Case study 11.2

DEFERMENT

'Did you know that on average around 15 per cent of most employers' telephone bills are in respect of private calls made by their employees?'

'No, really?'

'That's what our research tells us – I'll put a copy in the post for you to look through.'

'Thank you.'

'It's a pleasure and we can help you to cut that cost substantially.'

'Er . . .' (Respondent realises that he has swallowed the baited hook of the statistics of the wasted cost and given the caller the opportunity to reel him in. Now he frantically looks for a way to escape.)

'What I suggest we do is to arrange an appointment at a time suitable to you for one of our advisers to show you how your organisation can save thousands of pounds.'

'Well, I could be interested but not at the moment as I am so committed with the year end accounts [or something – it doesn't matter what – no-one will ever check up]. Please give me a ring towards the end of December [or another month at least four months away]. Thank you so much for calling, goodbye.'

Key technique

Cold callers are programmed (and often have a script designed) to keep the conversation going. Sentences which close the conversation down particularly if the word 'goodbye' is accompanied by the replacing of the receiver. Firmness tends to terminate the flow of the planned script, conversely any lack of firmness provides an opportunity for the cold caller to try again.

The determination of the call in Case Study 11.2 means that the contact may not actually have been terminated, but if the caller has any sense they will realise that conversion of this one may be difficult and it may be more cost-effective to try someone else. Of course, it may be worth ringing back in a few months.

Case study 11.3

SHUT UP

'Good afternoon, I am sure you will wish to know that we can help your organisation improve its sales by 20 per cent wouldn't you?'

'Not really. I am in the middle of a very complicated report and do not wish to be disturbed. Goodbye.'

Key technique

There is no such thing as a free gift. The response to the call may seem to border on the rude, but the response to that comment is that no-one asked the caller to make the call so what else do you expect when you cause an interruption? In some ways the original call was fairly rude as it assumes the respondent has nothing better to do than sit around in their office waiting to deal with cold callers.

Sadly, with some callers, one almost has to be rude to get rid of them as they can be very persistent, over-riding all attempts to close the conversation down. In many ways one can be attracted by the 'it's our policy retort' set out in Case Study 11.4 which can help avoid innumerable tricky calls.

Case study 11.4

IT'S AGAINST THE RULES

'Hallo Mrs Jones, I've got some great news regarding a new widget we are making available to selected customers at a special price before we go national.'

'Thank you for calling but our policy is not to deal with telephone sales. Goodbye.'

Key technique

Whilst brusque it is effective, although once a caller did manage to enquire 'why?' to which bait I nearly succumbed with an answer but remembered just in time and said 'We don't discuss company policy with outsiders either – goodbye.'

Those who experience frustration at the extent of cold calling and/or find great difficulty in fending off such unwanted callers may discover that they are about to gain powerful allies. In November 1995, the European Parliament voted to ban cold telephone calling throughout the European Community. Although this is subject to ratification it seems likely that the idea may progress. There is a wide range of opinion within the Community regarding the matter – in Germany and Luxembourg, for example, cold calling is already illegal.

Caller types

■ ■ ■

Most cold callers will be the extrovert type – they have to be in order to cope with the almost constant knock backs they receive from the majority of their calls. It takes a certain type of person to continue plugging away at a job which the majority of the population of the country find either at best irritating or at worst intrusive and patronising. An appreciation of the types may help arm ourselves for the encounter.

Aggressive

A minority, albeit a sizeable one, of cold callers can be downright aggressive even to the point of being rude. How they reconcile such an attitude with the requirement that they want the object of their aggression to become a customer or in some way part with money or time (or both) is somewhat perplexing. However, in many ways they pose the least problem in terms of 'fending off'. Most people in the UK are polite and courteous and may even be complimentary to one's face whilst seething with annoyance under the surface. The situation in the classic TV comedy 'Fawlty Towers' where the guests are all complaining amongst themselves but when the Basil, the hotel owner, asks them if everything is OK they reply that it is, may be exaggeration for the sake of humour, but equally it is not too far from the truth. By contrast Americans, French and Germans are nowhere near as reticent and as a result usually enjoy better service. It can be difficult to be rude, even when being truthful, to a party who is obsequious or ingratiating. Faced with rudeness and hostility, a similar reaction may be engendered which may bring the encounter to an abrupt end.

Case study 11.5

'NO, NO, NO, NO, NO'

The Agency was small and obtained its clients by word of mouth – that is personal recommendation. Experience had shown that widening the target audience by advertising did generate enquiries but most turned out to be unsatisfactory time-wasters. The magazine representative was trying to sell advertising space. The Agency patiently explained that the space was not for them. At this the representative started to lose his temper,

'But this is absurd. I am offering you space that we know will generate sales enquiries for you.'

'As I have explained most of those enquiries will waste our time.'

'I can't believe I am hearing this – you are a small agency – don't you want to grow?' [1]

'How we wish to manage our business is our affair.'

'Nonsense, everyone wants to grow – if you don't you go out of business.' [2]

'Well, that statement is partially untrue. In any event, there are many ways of existing and growing. Since I doubt if you know as much about our business as we do . . .'

(Interrupting) 'I know enough to know you don't know what you are talking about.' [3]

. . . (dialling tone as Agency owner hung up)

Key techniques

1 It is arguable that the phone could have been put down at this point. There is no reason, nor any excuse, for rudeness – and this is rudeness compounded by arrogant ignorance. If you are going to cold call successfully then you do need to know at least a little about the target's operation. The owner could have replied

   'I find you rude and see no point in continuing this conversation – goodbye.'

   As long as the phone is put down immediately the conversation should end. Some people make the mistake of saying the words but then hanging on to see what the caller will say next – it may be human nature to be curious but it does give the caller time to regroup and if (unlikely in the above type of encounter) the reaction is

   'Oh, I am terribly sorry, I didn't mean to be rude, I do beg your pardon'

   once again the British sense of fair play may surface and the conversation link may continue. The opportunity to end has been missed.

2 Now this has some basis in reason – businesses do not stand still – they must either grow or contract. However, in this context the caller is patronising the owner by inferring that he knows far more about the business than the person running it. In fact, of course, this could be true, but you are hardly going to win many friends by asserting or proving it! Once again the owner has the opportunity of closing the conversation since he can state quite reasonably that he finds the caller's attitude rude. He could quickly explain this as in **1** above or say 'Goodbye' and replace his receiver, or simply hang up.

3 Quite correctly this generates a conversation closer – once again the owner is being insulted by someone whose aim was to sell him some advertising space – an aim of which the caller lost sight very early on in the conversation.

176

Pleading

Once again it may be appropriate to consider initially the British character and in particular its inherent generosity. It has been suggested that as far as charity appeals are concerned there is no more generous nation in the world. Charity fund-raisers know this and can use it. Many charities now use telephone calling as a cost-effective way of raising money and very often this is successful. With larger companies even if they do not belong to the 1% Club (an association which aims to give around 1 per cent of its annual profit to charity each year), giving say £25 to each caller may be a cost-effective way of getting rid of the call – even assuming there is no genuine desire to aid the charity itself. However, for smaller organisations, particularly those still suffering from the recession and the fact that, in the UK and indeed in Europe, demand is likely to remain at not much above current levels at least into the next century, this may not be a practical method of dealing with the call. Understandably they will not wish to be rude or abusive (although such callers do receive this type of treatment on occasion).

177

Case study 11.6

COLD CHARITY

The small business was struggling having just lost one of its major customers. Things were obviously going to be very tight for at least the next year.

'Hallo Mrs Swift, its Della from United Charities, I wondered if we could put you down for the usual £50 donation this year?'

'I am awfully sorry Della but we simply have to cut out all expenditure that is not essential to the business – try me again next year – thanks for calling – bye.'

Key technique

In most conversations the caller holds the initiative, after all they have initiated the call. Here the businesswoman has taken the initiative away from the caller, she has been polite, given an indication that there may be some 'jam tomorrow' and closed the call all in one swift and short sentence. The essence of the close is speed – cold callers (not necessarily from charities) often try to retain the initiative. The respondent needs to insert his or her own sentence, close down the options and end the conversation (as shown in Case Study 11.1 above). This does need preparation and thus the best defence to cold calls is using closing down responses – that is being ready with your own script.

'Hallo, its Della from United Charities, I wondered if you could be so kind as to take one of our sponsored balloons in our next charity race? They only cost £25.'

'I am awfully sorry we've spent, in fact we've overspent, our charity budget for this year. I do wish you well with your appeal however, thanks for calling, bye.'

Once again, preparation and the all-embracing sentence wins the day. Yet the negative response has been provided with some degree of sympathy.

Note: In no way is this meant to be an argument for rebuffing charitable appeals. Realistically, however, there are so many such appeals that one may be forced by pure economics to rebuff some – but gently.

Going for the sympathy vote

This device entails trying to gain the sympathy of the target and create rapport in that way. It may be regarded as dangerous for the cold caller since the assertive and/or perceptive respondent may be able to force a better deal from the caller – or so they think.

Case study 11.7

LEGERDEMAIN

'Hallo Mr Sharp, it's Bert from Allied Panes – the double-glazing specialists – you may recall we spoke a few weeks ago.'

'Oh yes.' [1]

'I'm in real trouble – trade is so bad that I keep missing my targets and I've been told unless I hit my target this month I'm out of a job.'

'Oh dear.'

'I was wondering if I could tempt you to place the order we were talking about if I split my commission with you? It would help you as you'd get a better deal and it would help me get nearer my target and my job.'

'What price were you thinking of now?'

'Well, if you recall, we made it £2,377. I'll get around £250 commission on that so if I knock off say £127 we could call it £2,250.'

'Mmm . . . it's still too pricey – call it £2,150 and you've got a deal.'

'You drive a hard bargain – let me just look at a few figures. [pause] Oh alright then, I hope I don't run up against too many like you Mr Sharp.' [2]

Key techniques

1 Had Mr Sharp really wanted to end the conversation there and then he should have said

   'Oh yes I remember but I told you then that I was not interested and nothing has changed, thanks for calling, I must go, bye' which, using the continuous closing sentence technique effectively, closes the encounter down.

   179

2 Mr Sharp may feel that he has got a bargain and indeed he has saved £217 – just over 9 per cent of the price. However, some saving was always on given the opening gambit used by Bert. As a salesman of course Bert could be on far more than 9 per cent commission and almost certainly his company is prepared to fund some of the discount. Indeed they might have been prepared to go further – but both parties are probably satisfied. The moral may be never to take what is said at face value, and never to believe the sob story unless it can be proven!

Assertive

In many ways this last type of cold caller can be the most difficult to defend. They are never rude and so simply saying 'Goodbye' and/or replacing the receiver is unlikely to be an option without being rude oneself; they do not try for the sympathy of the respondent and they are seldom in the business of doing a special deal. They are simply very good at what they are doing. What is the secret of their skill? Their preparation tends to be meticulous, their script caters for every response they are likely to be given and they have a very good knowledge of their product or service. Above all, they probably understand the problems of the respondent and thus, by putting themselves in the position of the other person, gain insight into their reaction. In defending cold calls from such a source the respondent needs to adopt the same approach

- to understand what the assertive caller is all about (ie that they need to sell), and

- to realise that every standard response is likely to be countered by a programmed response (thus we will need either to seize the initiative or to counter the spiel with an original response).

180

Case study 11.8

ONLY PREPARATION CAN DEFEND

The businessman was up to his eyes in work when the phone rang.

'Hallo Mr Stonewall, your Mr Buckpasser suggested I give you a ring to fix up a time when it would be convenient for you to see our new superwidget.' [1]

'I'm not sure that we are in the market for your superwidget.' [2]

'I appreciate your concern but I must tell you that 40 per cent of the top companies who are producing your products are moving to the superwidget and you don't want to be left behind do you?' [3]

'No, er . . . [4]

'So when can we come along and demonstrate how effective it is and how your operation can benefit from it?' [5]

'I'm not sure. . . er . . . ' [6]

'Tell you what – I'm only just down the road from you at the moment. I'll pop along straightaway and leave it with you so you can inspect it at your leisure.' [7]

'But I'm . . . ' [8]

'Don't worry, I'll know where you are – it'll only take a few moments anyway – see you later, bye.' [9]

Key techniques

1 The cold caller has used some of the devices suggested in Chapter Ten and has added the inference that the superwidget is something that Mr Stonewall's company simply cannot do without.

2 CLANG. Saying 'I'm not sure' indicates uncertainty which could be used to argue that you might be interested after all.

3 This demonstrates that the salesman knows something of the industry and also uses the device of the rhetorical question to force the answer 'No' (few organisations want to be left behind or at least for it to be known that they want to be left behind).

4 CLANG. Mr Stonewall is being sucked into the programmed spiel. He should have said

'Yes, I know, but our market is more specialised and we neither want nor need to keep up with our market leaders.'

5 The cold caller has got where he wanted. The inference from this question is that he is responding to an invite from Mr Stonewall to put himself out to show the superwidget to him – the ball is now firmly in Mr Stonewall's court to suggest a date to someone of whom he had never heard until a couple of minutes previously.

6 CLANG. Once again any indecision provides an instant peg on which the cold caller can hang his next link in the chain using which he will pull himself into the organisation. Responding as follows would be better

'I'm sorry I have no time to see items which are of purely speculative interest. If you would care to send me the specification for the superwidget I'll have our people look at it and, if it has any potential for us, I'll get back to you – you have our address don't you? . . .'

The cold caller has had the rhetorical question device turned upon him – he can hardly answer 'No' and in any event Mr Stonewall hardly pauses before continuing with the continuing closing sentence

'. . . now if you will excuse me I must get back to my work, thank you for calling, goodbye.'

7 This is very persuasive since the cold caller is inferring that he will just pop in, leave the widget so that Mr Stonewall can have a look at it when he has some time and go. What will happen is that the cold caller will visit the company having inveigled this 'invitation'

181

and the company will then find it even harder to dislodge him from the premises than they are finding it to dislodge him from the phone.

8   CLANG. He who hesitates is lost – any hesitation or break in the flow gives the cold caller a chance to slip a further sentence in. Mr Stonewall would (had he not, as he should, already closed the conversation using previous devices) have been better to have stated

'No, don't do that, you'll simply be wasting your time. I'm just leaving for our other office in any event. Just send the specification – it's extremely unlikely that we will be interested. Thank you for calling – goodbye.'

9   That's torn it. Having failed to stop the progress towards this aim of the 'foot in the door', Mr Stonewall (unless he really does rush out of the office) is now almost forced to see the cold caller. The cold caller has inferred that his visit will only take a few moments (which is extremely unlikely as he will now try and develop the whole selling spiel) when he was actually referring to it only taking a short time for him to get from wherever he was calling from to the target office. Using a mobile phone of course he could have been parked outside all the time – even blocking Mr Stonewall's escape route.

Warning: The trouble is, of course, that at the back of his mind Mr Stonewall might have the sneaking suspicion that the superwidget might actually be very useful for his business if only he could consider it in peace and without being put under pressure by the salesman. Cold callers need to appreciate that many respondents can be in this position – playing it their way may be more productive than applying too much pressure.

In this scenario, if his stonewalling is effectual, Mr Stonewall could be compared to General Custer refusing to see a salesman trying to sell him the Gatling gun (the earliest machine gun) and instead going out to fight an overwhelming number of Indians with single shot rifles, knives and bayonets. If there is this niggle at the back of your mind perhaps the response

'I do not intend discussing this over the phone, send me a fax on the subject and I'll have a look and get back to you if we are interested.'

Could be an effective let down since the use of the fax infers that it will gain some attention which a letter may not.

Suggested 'stonewalling' sentences

1 *'I am sure your product is excellent but I have no budget.'*

2 *'We have a number of different developments at the moment and may be moving in a different direction.'*

3 *'Yes, I have heard reports of it but we have decided it is not for us.'*
   (To the immediate reply *'can I ask what/why that is'* reply *'I'm afraid that's confidential'*.)

4 *'Our company policy is not to buy from telephone selling – please send me a brochure, goodbye.'*

5 *'We only buy on recommendations from our trade association.'*
   (You may not get many bouquets from them if the cold caller then pesters them for a recommendation, of course!)

6 *'Sorry can't discuss it now, I'm*

   – *late for a meeting'*

   – *in a meeting'*

   – *on my way to see the Chairman'*

   – *in an interview'*

   – *just off on holiday'*

   – *just back from holiday and snowed under'*

   and so on.

If you really want to frighten someone away say *'I'm just going to see our Receivers'*. The inference that the organisation is in financial difficulties may frighten away some unwanted cold callers (since it infers that it might be unlikely that they will receive payment) could also destroy the reputation of your business. Of course, that assumes that the caller knows what is meant by the term which is a dangerous assumption as many placing such calls are considerably inexperienced in business matters.

7 '*Sorry, we're not able to place any orders now*

- *we have a buying freeze on*'

- *we have a cash flow problem*'

(this may not be as severe as referring to Receivers but it should send some signals to the cold caller that even if he achieves the sale, being paid for it may be delayed)

- *we don't buy over the phone*'

- *we don't buy from companies unless we have two satis-factory trade references from them.*'

8 '*I can't possibly talk to you about this*

- *it's nothing to do with me*'

- *it's not my responsibility*'

- *I know nothing about your company or products.*'

In truth of course, it may be that you are just not interested in the product or the selling company or the salesman and it might be better to tell the truth

- '*I'm simply not interested, goodbye.*'

The cold caller may be absolutely certain in his or her mind that their product is absolutely right for you and your organisation and their job is not necessarily to sell the product as to convince you that you have a real need for it. The dividing line between genuine belief that the product is right for you and patronising the respondent by inferring that the cold caller knows more about the requirements of their business than they do, is very thin.

Warning: Although you may have read this Chapter and have prepared yourself to man the ramparts and defend yourself against the machinations of the cold caller, don't overlook the fact that someone else may answer your phone. Your secretary, personal assistant, etc., (particularly the temporary versions of such employees helping out whilst the permanent occupants are on holiday) also need to be briefed to ensure that, however unwittingly, they do not commit you.

It may be helpful for all involved in fielding cold calls to

- have all the above responses handy near the phone
- customise the above and add to them with any additional items they can conjure up, and
- say each of them out loud and tape the performance.

Repelling the persistent cold caller may be as much about the tone you use (positive, controlled, determined) as the words that are used.

185

12

Temper, temper – 'When thou art angry all our days are gone'

Key learning points

1 Losing one's temper hands the initiative and control of a tough call to the other party (unless they also lose their temper in which case any resolution is likely to be impossible).

2 Despite provocation it is essential to deal with such callers with patience and tact – albeit with firmness.

3 Recognition of the various types of callers and determining the type of reaction can aid the defusing of tough calls.

4   In dealing with the media it is essential to be well-briefed and to practise answering the slanted questions that may be asked.

Lose your temper – lose the argument
■ ■ ■

Rational thought and argument disappear when temper rules and most people seized by temper start to exaggerate and make wild statements bearing neither relation to the facts nor to reality. This is very much a factor of the use of the phone. Most of us are susceptible to finding ourselves carried away by our own rhetoric. By speaking very quickly (which tends to be a product of a loss of temper) we will find we can use an astonishing number of words – not always words that we might have wanted to use. Conversely it is far more difficult, though not impossible, particularly if using a word processor, e-mail or electric typewriter, to lose one's temper when writing though one will certainly lose the effect of the tone which can itself add to the ire being demonstrated. Great self-control is essential to ensure that temper is met by calmness, exaggeration by close adherence to the facts and loud shouting by a quiet tone.

Case study 12.1

AGGRAVATION RILES – AND LOSES

Just before he left for a tribunal case the consultant was telephoned by his opposite number in a fair degree of anger. The papers his opposite number had sent to the tribunal had been mislaid and insufficient copies were available to allow the tribunal to sit.

'I insist that you bring additional sets with you.'

'Really – why is that?'

'You're the defendant, the onus is on you to bring them – you make sure you do.'

'I'm sorry but I don't understand the point you are making and I should be obliged if you would stop shouting as I can't understand everything you're saying.'

'I'll shout if I want to – you just get those papers to the tribunal.'

'The papers I take it are the bundle that your side put in.'

'Well, of course they are, what the hell do you think we've been talking about all this time.'

'That bundle, like this case, was your client's responsibility and I suggest you ask him to make sure that if they have gone missing they are replaced.'

Key technique

The suggestion that calmness and quietness be used as the counter to temper is valid, but it must be noted that in some instances such a response can actually further inflame the situation. That is unfortunate but the loser is the person who has lost their temper. In the above instance the barrister seemed so annoyed by the encounter that he seemed to slacken his grip on the case and it was lost.

Provocation

Even when acting under provocation temper loss is almost certainly likely to be counter-productive since facts tend to be submerged under the exchange. Patience is everything. In *Thinking on Your Feet in Negotiations*, Jane Hodgson recalls hearing someone on the radio state 'the Chinese are past masters at negotiation – they are resourceful, patient and ruthless' but having considered the quote further, she concluded that good negotiators should certainly be resourceful and patient, but firm rather than ruthless.

189

Case study 12.2

JUSTIFIABLE ANGER ALL BUT LOSES THE POINT

The Manager was furious that after considerable and protracted delays the agent with whom he was dealing seemed determined to avoid advising either him or his company on matters seriously affecting his company's unit. Twice in four weeks, letters supposedly sent to him had 'gone astray', the lack of advice thereby wasting time that could have been used to protect the position.

He telephoned the agent and initially received an off-hand response. This included two or three comments that were incorrect and a derisory dismissal of the Manager's assertions that the matter had been dragging on for over two years. Unfortunately the Manager then lost his temper, as then did the agent. The ensuing slanging match was terminated after a few irate minutes by both parties slamming down their respective phones.

The Manager then cooled down and faxed a letter setting out the evidence of his company's case, including the non-arrival of the two letters, and added copies of the correspondence originated by a colleague of the existing agent, evidencing that the matter had indeed been going on for over two years. He concluded his letter by regretting the outburst but hoped the recital of all the matters would show the company's justifiable case. The agent telephoned back with a complete apology, explaining that he was dealing with two companies with the same name and had confused the two in the heat of the moment!

Having cleared the air, the two were able to build a relationship based on understanding, in the interests of which the Manager decided that it might be unwise to press for an explanation for the non-delivery of the two letters that had actually sparked the row!

190

Key technique

It can be very difficult to explain one's case over the phone – the points can be constantly interrupted and the thrust of the arguments pushed off course. With complicated matters it may be better to put contentions down in writing and send or fax them first, stating that you will ring the target subsequently to discuss matters. This should minimise the likelihood of a tricky call.

Watching the ripples

Earlier I referred to a remark from Virgin Atlantic that if a customer has a bad flight he or she is likely to tell 17 other people – all potential fliers and customers. 'No caller is an island' (to misquote John Donne) and a bad experience with a supplier (or equivalent) can have quite unexpected effects – basically you never know who is listening or to whose ears a problem may be brought.

Case study 12.3

THE CUSTOMER IS ALWAYS WRONG

This was the second order placed by the customer. The first had been a somewhat rushed order for Christmas gifts and the second was in response to a discount flier the company had produced to try and generate trade in the low demand part of the year. Following its standard practice, the company had produced and invoiced 10 per cent over the number of items ordered. The customer telephoned to query this.

'I am very surprised to see that the order which I requested for delivery by 1st April was delivered late without any apology and in addition you have charged me for overs.'

'Yes sir, that is in accordance with our standard conditions of trade shown in our catalogue – I'll send you a copy.' [1]

After receiving the catalogue, the customer telephoned again.

'I queried your charging for the overs on my second order, and the late delivery, and you have sent me your catalogue. However, I would point out that your discount flier makes no reference to any such conditions. In addition, you have ignored the fact that the order was delivered late, whilst, in reading through the catalogue, I have realised that you overcharged my first order last Christmas, as you charged for overprinting which is not referred to for the goods I ordered.' [2]

'I am sorry to hear you are unhappy with the company [3a], our offer sheet was rushed out and we overlooked the requirement to refer to our terms, we will be mindful of this in future to avoid any such remote misunderstandings [3b]. I'll send you a credit note for the cost of the overs. Please accept my unequivocal apologies for the late delivery, which under any circumstances should not have occurred [3c].'

'But what about this overcharging on my first order?'

'You are correct in identifying a discrepancy in our catalogue. Unfortunately this was noticed after the printing had been completed.'

'You mean you sent out catalogues knowing there was an error?'

'Well, it was felt our customers would appreciate that even though it does not state this, the additional charge would apply [3d]. I think it is unreasonable of you to stress this point [3e]. We hope that with this explanation you will feel more sympathetic towards us and the efforts we make on behalf of our customers [3f].'

'I note all that and accept that mistakes do happen, but when they do, the correct course of action is for the company to accept responsibility, not to try to evade it.'

'But there was no deliberate attempt to mislead you – yours is the only query that has been raised regarding the charge for overprinting – and we feel it is unreasonable. We would appreciate your settling our account.'
[4] & [5]

Key techniques

1 Treating a genuine customer query in this dismissive way, as well as ignoring one of the points raised, merely stores up trouble for the future.

2 The irritation caused by the dismissive approach is the direct cause of the customer investigating further. The company must either try to justify the three matters, or negotiate (rather than impose) a way out of it.

3 This dismissive response seeks refuge from the facts in unnecessary and totally 'flowery' wording, the effect of which is merely irritating. Plain language without jargon, flattery or 'flowery' phrases is preferable and more effective. What has happened here has been a complete disregard for the KISS technique and as a result the semiotic message 'I can con you with some impressive language so that you will not press your point' is being sent to the customer. It might work with some – with others, and particularly the kind of person that has picked up the point that the company is in breach of its published terms, it is merely an added irritant.

In addition, the comments slide round the facts – the customer had a genuine grievance which, despite all the words, has not actually been answered. He was not unhappy with the company [3a], but he is unhappy (and probably becoming unhappier by the jargon-filled sentence) with its unprofessional service, particularly as he is being forced to waste time trying to sort out its mistakes. This makes the last comment [3f] totally illogical. Since it is the customer who has suffered, why should the company [3e] expect sympathy? By its own admissions [3b, c & d], the company is in the wrong in each case.

4 This is a response which could work although there is considerable risk of it coming unstuck. No-one has stated the mistake was

deliberate, whilst reasonableness is an opinion which the two parties are unlikely to share. Whether the customer believes his was
the only query is irrelevant – it is a real query and a real overcharge
to him, and arises from the contract between him and the company. However, the onus is now with the customer regarding the
settling of the account. If he fails to settle at all, the company could
take legal action to recover, with all the attendant inconvenience
and costs (which in the circumstances it is unlikely to recover), but
it does leave the customer the option of deducting the disputed
amount from the account when settling it, which would then place
the onus for further action on the company. Conversely, the customer, since the order was delivered late, could insist that the
company take the whole order back, which is the last thing the
company would want.

5 The company failed to appreciate its goal and lost sight of
the desired result. The result should have been satisfaction
of the customer when raising a legitimate matter of concern,
and avoidance of a returned and wasted order. A more positive
approach initially would have saved an annoyance turning into a
legal dispute.

6 Of course the company may have been aware of the weakness of
its own case and decided to be deliberately obtuse hoping the
customer would lose his temper which would allow them to pick
holes in any exaggeration which would then by association
damage the validity of the other points.

Postscript: The customer was bemused to find exactly the same
wording repeated in the company's catalogue for the following year
and reported the matter to the Trading Standards Office.

It really doesn't have to be like that. Positive thought and
planning can go a long way towards avoiding tough calls
and providing good customer service (which itself will
reduce the very incidence of such calls). Remember the way
the Medes and the Persians used to make their decisions –
once when drunk and a second time when sober. Perhaps
the advice we can derive from their ancient civilisation is
that we should do nothing when seized by temper but wait
until we have cooled down.

Got it taped

If it is dangerous speaking in anger on the phone it is even more dangerous to leave messages on an answerphone when one has lost one's temper. In conversation and on the phone, so many words may be said it can be difficult to remember what was and was not said. Accordingly it may be possible to deny some of what was said and thus to minimise the damage to one's case. But if the words said in temper are caught by tape on an answerphone they cannot be denied because a physical record exists.

Case study 12.4

NO USE DENYING IT . . .

The agency had placed a young foreign woman with an English family. Within a few hours of her arrival the mother of the woman phoned the agency to say she was not happy. The agency pointed out that they needed to deal with the woman direct and phoned her. It seemed that her mother had exaggerated her comments and there was little wrong. Two weeks later the agency, on opening the office, found a confused, angry and semi-hysterical message on their answerphone from the woman's mother stating that the family had thrown her out, that it was all the agency's fault and that she was reporting them for dereliction of duty.

The agency phoned the English family and found that, without letting on to the family, the young woman was leaving them and trying to do so before they discovered she had gone. She had simply decided that the type of work was not suitable for her.

The agency were then placed in the situation of combating someone who whilst seized by temper was making all sorts of threats. The director took the tape and made a transcript. He then composed a letter in which he took each point made on the tape and set out the facts. The letter was sent to the woman's mother with a copy to the authorities to which she was threatening to report the agency.

Key technique

The value of the tape was incalculable since there was physical evidence of what had been said. Had it all been said in a conversation at least half of it would probably have been forgotten and in any event could have been denied as false, faulty interpretation or deliberate misunderstanding.

Thinking time

∎ ∎ ∎

As well as the advantage of providing a physical record of what was said, the other great advantage of using an answerphone, particularly when taking a call from someone who has lost their temper, is that it provides thinking time during which one can consider how best to deal with the problem. Often when in the middle of a tough call we can be forgiven for wishing that we had a control by activating which we could stop the world to provide time to think of alternative courses of action. This is where it is essential that if time for thought is required, it is obtained by firmly stating that there has to be a break for such consideration. Of course, if expecting calls which could require thinking time, it is not beyond the bounds of reasonableness to use an answerphone to answer all our calls. Monitoring the calls in this way allows us to answer them if we wish to ('sorry I came back in the office just as the phone rang') and to think about the messages relating to the calls we do not wish to answer.

Dealing with the types

∎ ∎ ∎

We have already identified certain types of cold callers but of course there are others with whom we need to interface who are not trying to press us to buy goods or services we would prefer to be without. The suggested 'ways to deal' are merely ideas – not absolutes – as there can rarely be a 'best' way as nearly every situation is different – 'circumstances alter cases'.

Recognising tough callers

Stallers – people who find it difficult to make decisions. In many ways such people may not be too difficult to deal with since the alternative decisions can be put to them and left with them. Since their problem is making the decision at least this should provide an opportunity for a re-think if necessary. If trying to help them, we may need to find out the reason for their indecisiveness.

Agreeables – people who agree on the phone but then change their mind subsequently. This can be frustrating as it will seem that you have sorted everything only to find out that it's all up in the air again. Try to spot them during the telephone call and pin them down once and for all. Having said that, tricky call fielders should have some sympathy with them as they too might need time to reconsider the situation and their initial agreement to a solution may be merely a device to buy thinking time for reconsideration.

Limpets – people who have a problem but refuse to discuss it or to go away. The tricky call fielder will need to use all their guile to try and prise out of them the nature of the problem – pointing out that only if they open up can their problem be dealt with.

Pessimists – these people do not believe that anything can be done to resolve their problem and with that attitude they are probably correct as they will endeavour to make sure it doesn't work. However, the plan should be to get them to determine their worst case and then try to solve or provide suggestions for solving that.

Big heads – people who know everything – including all there is to know about customer care and telephone trickiness. A super-professional approach is necessary. Their conceit should also be pandered to. Phrases such as 'as I am sure you are aware' or 'as you know' may help.

Complaint specialists – will know, because they spend a great deal of their time complaining, how to exploit the system to gain the maximum benefit. If they have a case, no matter how tenuous, it may be better to pay them off simply to be rid of what could become a lengthy dispute.

All-out hostility specialist – the person who is aggressive, may have lost their temper and is determined not just to win the encounter but to humiliate their opponent. Indeed, the fact that they regard the respondent as an opponent says a great deal about their attitude. It is essential in dealing with someone like this that all facts are discovered and if possible agreed, that calmness despite provocation is adhered to, that alternative suggestions for solutions are put forward and that every aspect of the problem is examined so that the person cannot re-open the encounter once it seems to have been settled.

197

Dealing with the media

■ ■ ■

Many organisations are of considerable interest to the media – they are newsworthy and should an event occur – particularly bad news – then the media will want information. Unfortunately very often the interest will be more from the need to fill column inches or air time than for genuine interest in the subject matter and thus responsible reporting may be sublimated in the interest of the shocking or the mass market appeal. Organisations need to plan for such interest and a checklist may be helpful.

DRAFT MEDIA COMMUNICATION POLICY

General

1 The organisation recognises the natural interest that will be evinced by the media in its operations and will make all information, other than that which is regarded as confidential, regularly available.

---

2 [Name and deputy] will act as spokesperson for the organisation and will be briefed continually by those responsible for each [division, product, etc.].

3 In the event of other employees being contacted by media representatives, they will always be referred to the spokesperson.

4 In interfacing with the media, the spokesperson will endeavour to be truthful at all times, and to ensure that information is correctly reported.

5 All media contacts will be regularly briefed so that they have background knowledge of the organisation, updated continuously.

6 In the event of a serious occurrence the senior manager responsible must brief the spokesperson as quickly as possible so that he in turn is ready to answer media questions.

Research

No briefing or interview will be successful unless adequate preparation and research has been carried out. Thus, the following are necessary:

1 Identify the areas of operation in which the media could be interested.

2 Identify the target audiences and the information they will be seeking.

3 Establish who is to deal with the ongoing enquiry and how they are to be briefed and updated concerning progress and all related aspects.

4 Encourage the spokesperson to create links with media representatives, establishing names, positions, main interests or 'angles', deadlines, bias, and so on.

5 Examine all stories and reports concerning the organisation and its products to ensure the correct image is being created, attempting to use the contacts to correct false impressions.

6 Continually develop questions, and answers thereto, that the company least wants asked and become conversant with both, updated as necessary.

7 Prepare and update a resumé of all the successes of the company so that good news is available to leaven the bad.

Crisis reaction

Whilst briefing the media on the more mundane aspects of company performance may be relatively easy, dealing with such interest in the aftermath of a calamity or disaster, poses considerable problems. These may be capable of being tackled only if based on contingency planning – that is anticipating the disaster and making plans in advance that can deal with anticipated effects. The advantage of 'planning for disaster' is that lengthy and calm thought can be given to alternative tactics and reactions, without the considerable time pressure for reaction that the incidence of disaster can cause. In addition, consideration of alternative actions in the event of disaster, may suggest beneficial changes in current operations. Obviously if it is to be of value such planning must be both comprehensive and regularly updated.

Checklist: Crisis reaction

1 Initial contact will usually be by telephone. A person should be nominated, possibly the Company Secretary, though there should always be one or two back up personnel to handle initial queries if the spokesperson is not available.

2 Keep calm and listen to what the inquirer is asking.

3 Make notes of, or tape, the call content, time, the caller's name, position and media represented, the caller's telephone number and location.

4 Do not respond to questions, comments, observations – simply make notes as set out in **3** above and state that by a (stated) time someone will respond either in a press release or by telephone, and so on.

5 Do NOT be flustered by indications of deadlines, insistence on immediate response, outrageous accusations, or innuendo.

6 By the time promised, not less than an hour, ensure someone does ring the caller back with comments.

7 Keep responses, press statements, and so on, short. Embroidery can both offset the punch effect and provide other 'angles' from which the reporter can come back at the author.

8 Provide a contact name/number.

9 Should such contact be used then the above guidelines should be applied. If necessary the spokesperson should ring back after taking time for thought.

> **10** If press releases are used, these need to be drafted carefully so that
>
> - the essential features of the news to be reported is contained in the first paragraph
>
> - the news must be of substance and presented concisely and clearly
>
> - it provides quotable quotes from named authorities, and
>
> - it specifies a realistic release date and gives an in-house contact and telephone number.

When an incident occurs or an interview is sought, particularly over the phone, immediate response is necessary to ensure the items covered by the checklist below are addressed. In this way whoever has to deal with tough calls from the media should be prepared for such calls and be able to fend off any pointed questions.

Media spokesperson checklist

1 As comprehensive and complete a brief as possible must be prepared. Organisation data, performance, products, problems, plans and so on, must be available and updated.

2 The point or aim of the interview must be discovered and appropriate responses and statements prepared particularly if these are likely to be controversial or embarrassing.

3 The spokesperson needs to have total control of the brief, of all facts and of the prepared responses, and to be able to speak knowledgeably concerning the subject matter. Any hesitation, lack of confidence or inadequate knowledge will be communicated to the listener or viewer and create doubt of veracity. In this respect it may be better to admit 'I don't know' rather than to try to 'flannel' through an answer.

4 Three or four simple messages that the organisation wishes to promote must be developed, possibly with

'changes of direction' sentences, so that if the interviewer leads off in one direction, the spokesperson may be able to return it to the company's preferred message. This approach needs to be controlled since a constant 'refusal' to answer the question may lead to a far more inquisitive or confrontational interview.

5 The spokesperson must be ready for the 'off the cuff' and unrehearsed question deliberately introduced and designed to catch him unawares to lead him to make an unprepared or unwise comment or answer.

6 Above all the spokesperson must be able to keep calm under pressure and/or goading, to be able to think quickly to fend off or deflect aggression and criticism, to retain control, and never to lose their temper.

7 The spokesperson must recognise that most live media interviews last a minute or less and thus it may be possible only to get across two or three authoritative comments. Trying to deal with a number of points, particularly if some are relatively trivial may detract from the important points.

8 The spokesman needs to be calm, alert and interested and serious, but not humorous, flustered, or flippant. (To some extent, the way a message is delivered can be more effective than the content.)

9 Take time to think about the questions, asking for them to be repeated if necessary.

10 False statements should not be allowed to pass unchecked, the record should be corrected.

11 Be positive not defensive. It may be better to 'own up' to a bad performance or event with a promise to 'improve' or rectify, rather than trying to defend an untenable position. The latter alternative will normally display the company in a poor light regardless of the circumstances and the impression will be 'they have learned nothing from the mistake', so nothing will change. This is particu-

larly important when there has been loss, injury or death. It is essential that genuine sympathy is expressed.

Case study 12.5

PREPARATION HELPS

John Howard of PMS International needs to deal with the press on a regular basis. As an experienced public relations manager he has passed the need for checklists like the above as they are a matter of habit. However, his phone is linked to a tape recorder and all telephone calls to the press are taped so that there is a record of exactly what was said should a dispute ensue.

13

■ ■ ■

Phoning the future

Key learning points

1   The growth of teleworking and use of e-mail poses communication problems which require users to rethink the way they use technology.

2   Imprecise use of words, and particularly the use of jargon needs to be avoided to try and keep the messages clear and understandable.

3   E-mail is often used without thinking sufficiently about the effect of the words being used.

4   The language of the future may use internationally recognised symbols as well as words to try and ensure comprehension of the exact meaning required.

The future is ephemeral
■ ■ ■

Just over 100 years ago virtually no-one knew what a telephone was let alone guessed its extraordinary potential in terms of global and even extra-global communication. The past century has seen the exploitation of Bell's invention in a way which nobody could have foreseen, as telecommunication has penetrated most of the globe. Obviously there is still scope for the development of such systems where so far they have not penetrated but for many, to whom the telephone may appear as somewhat 'old hat', the future in terms of telecommunication lies within the use of computer networks to convey messages and to access information. Linking computers to one another so that like a net they can 'talk' to each other has been around for over 20 years but it is only in approximately the last five years that the concept and practice of the information superhighway has caught the imagination of the mass market. The fact that two subscribers can now communicate via their keyboards without either leaving their chairs has attracted many people around the world. It was estimated in 1993 that there were then around 50 million subscribers to the World Wide Web (WWW) in 152 countries around the world. According to a survey commissioned by PhoneLinK in 1994, although there is substantial use of the Internet for accessing information (40 per cent of users) and transferring files (50 per cent of users) no less than 88 per cent of operators use it simply for e-mailing other operators. The WWW is seeing its traffic increase at a phenomenal rate – it increased ten fold in 1994 alone. The Web allows users to access around 5,000 databases throughout the world, of which about 10 per cent are in the UK – all for the price of a local phone call in addition to a subscription to the network services.

The virtual office

■ ■ ■

With the Web in place and now growing in terms of depth rather than width of coverage (since it already covers most of the world), it provides a service whereby a lone operator sitting in his or her own home, can research information, converse electronically with a contact or expert on the far side of the world, call down data, check references and supply information to all callers – and even pay for the service which has been used provided they have a credit card. It is thus possible to operate a whole business from one's own chair. Ignoring the understandable human need to interrelate to other human beings, man being a gregarious creature, it is possible to imagine that much of the work undertaken and wealth created in the 21st century will actually be generated in this way – by individual users accessing, contributing to and drawing data and information from their homes. Some enthusiastic journalists have suggested that unless a business is linked to the Internet within the next few years they will not be in business by the year 2020. This may be an exaggeration, although few businesses can see 25 years ahead in any event, but nevertheless the changes wrought by technology will be immense and should not be underestimated. Two hundred years ago the industrial revolution in the UK attracted people from the country into the towns and cities in search of work. It is not impossible to visualise a situation in far less than 200 years hence (even 20?) where a considerable proportion of the population has reverted to being spread far more thinly throughout the whole country as the need to congregate to find work and to carry on work disappears. A fair degree of this kind of remote teleworking is already in existence and some of the lack of effectiveness of, for instance, the transport strikes of 1995 may be attributed to the fact that using a personal computer, modem and telephone link many employees who would otherwise have travelled into their offices in towns and cities, remained at home and worked from there. British Telecom (BT) estimates that in 1995 there were nearly three million people working from home in the UK and according to the Henley Centre this figure is likely to reach 10 million by the year 2000. If this is correct then it would mean that nearly half the workforce of the country would then be teleworking on either a full or part time basis. As Iain Vallance, chairman of BT, stated 'teleworking is rather like going to work on the telephone line rather than the Piccadilly Line' and if it catches on the way it is predicted one beneficial effect will be that it will be far more pleasant to use the Piccadilly Line!

It requires only for increasing numbers of such employees to gain a taste for a perceived freer life where they save at least the time (as well as the cost and aggravation) of commuting for teleworking to really take off. It is difficult to imagine the spin off effects of commuters in effect becoming computers (or at least computer operators), but already substantial numbers are doing just that. They may be able to communicate via their computers but inevitably they will also need (if only to relieve the silence and hear another human voice) to use the phone. Whilst operating on different bases, phone and computer link are essentially the same – posing the same problems that have been addressed in this book. E-mail, however, poses some new problems and again these need to be addressed if the system is to work effectively.

E-mail
■ ■ ■

Electronic mailing is effected by typing a message on a computer screen and affixing the electronic address of the recipient to the message. By pressing the send key the message is transmitted electronically to the recipient and appears on their screen or is held pending display at will. It is, in normal events, much faster than the normal mail (often described by e-mail devotees as 'snail mail') and certainly cheaper, as the cost of the message is merely the equivalent of a local phone call since it is routed via the shortest net link between the sender's computer and the recipient's computer. The National Science Foundation estimated in 1994 that over 10 billion e-mail messages are now sent during a year.

The use and potential of the Internet is outside the scope of this book, although it is fascinating to note that romance can blossom and flourish in cyberspace. A librarian in Canada formed a link via the net with a librarian in Australia. Using the net they corresponded electronically for several months and eventually one proposed to the other in the same way. Similarly, American policewoman Donna Qalawi 'met' Craig Bottomley, a print shop manager from Newcastle, on the 'highway'. Having spent 100 hours 'calling' Donna and Craig then exchanged faxes and phone calls and are now married.

Leaving aside the potentially glamorous (and apparently romantic) world of international interfacing, we can in our own organisations use e-mail to try to aid internal communication. The operative word, however, is 'try'. Since the fact that we have a speedy process at our fingertips of itself does not necessarily mean that communication will improve – indeed the reverse may be true. In the early part of this book, we considered the barriers to communication that exist generally and particularly in relation to the use of the phone. The point was made that compared to face to face communication the telephone can actually be an imperfect communication device. If we lose 40 per cent of our communicative power when we are not face to face with our target then automatically communication is almost doubly difficult than it would otherwise have been. So how does this apply when we relate it to e-mail?

Firstly, we have an advantage with e-mail in that our words can actually appear in front of the recipient. There should be no reason for the actual words not to be remembered as they are there in front of him or her, and the recipient can print a record. It will be difficult subsequently for the recipient to infer that (s)he does not remember a particular item being said as can happen if referring to a telephone call.

207

Secondly, we have an advantage that we can marshal and present all our thoughts and arguments without being interrupted by anyone as we would were we face to face and trying to assemble certain facts and contentions. Conversation tends to be somewhat 'tangential' – if we do not interrupt ourselves with new thoughts then the listener may well interrupt us and before we know where we are we are well away from the subject we wished to raise. However, if we are going to transmit our message via e-mail we have the advantage that no-one can interrupt us – the message can get through unscathed.

Did I just say advantage? Like many aspects of the problem of communication this is two-edged – yes, our target will have a permanent record but if we have not thought out carefully what we want to send, or we have sent it whilst angry or annoyed then the permanence of the words may come back to haunt us. Obviously this did not happen with the two librarians or the police sergeant and the print shop manager whose romantic interludes were referred to above, but the point there is that both couples corresponded electronically over a period of time and this would allow them to get to know and understand the way in which each other wrote and thus thought. If we communicate regularly whether by written, visual or verbal means ultimately we gain an insight into the approach of the other party. It is estimated that many married couples actually talk to each other for less than 15 minutes each day – this does not mean that they are not communicating. Because they know each other well they can communicate virtually without talking – demeanour, body position, general attitude as much as words or tone can, when one knows another intimately, be as effective a means of communication as a 500 word speech summarising feelings – indeed the former is probably a more accurate guide. Words can mean different things to different people and words said without thinking, without an appreciation of the way in which they will be taken by the other party, and so on, can be a bar against rather than a means towards communication. Indeed, a careless use of a word can give completely the wrong impression and create a problem where none existed previously.

Case study 13.1

WATER PROBLEMS

In the super heat summer of 1995 (the hottest in the UK for over 200 years) the consumer filling his kettle noticed that the water seemed very cloudy. He let the tap run and tried again, using a long glass so that he could see more clearly. The water remained very cloudy. Bearing in mind that there had previously been a number of problems in the London area with water supplies being infected by toxic organisms, he rang the emergency number for the water company.

'Our water supply seems to be very cloudy.'

'Have you tried running the tap for some time?.'

'Yes, and it is still the same.'

'Our workmen have been in your area today so it is probably air in the water.'

'Would air make the supply cloudy?'

'It could do – but there's no need to panic.'

209

Key technique

'Panic?' – who said anything about panicking? The water company spokesperson had not been properly briefed in the terms of the use of certain words in communicating with customers. Here 'panic' was both inaccurate and inadvisable since

- it generated an instinctive and negative reaction from a consumer who was effecting what he thought was a responsible act of asking before using – effectively he felt he was being patronised

- the word itself is emotive and could create a feeling that the situation was more serious than it was – one where panic might be appropriate!

Case study 13.2

ANCIENT HISTORY

Whilst not suggesting that before surfing the information highway a subscriber needs to sober up like the Medes and Persians of old, the point is that as soon as we have typed the message and the address and tapped the 'send' key, our message is beyond recall and can be instantly with the recipient, warts and all, bad phrases as well as good, inadequate language and poor meaning. With instantaneous transmission at our fingertips we need to be very careful that what we send is what we really want to send and a few hours reflection may make all the difference to the way our message is received and its overall effectiveness.

Key technique

Just like the phone call, the effect of our facial expression is lacking and something meant as a joke or light-hearted aside may be taken seriously and before we know it we have a row on our hands when none was intended.

Surely, one can argue, this is no different to writing a letter? To some extent that is true. However, often the originators of an e-mail message would, had they written instead, dictated the letter to a secretary, or drafted it themselves on-screen. From either source they would have then seen a hard copy which they would be expected to read and sign before consigning it to the Post Office. Thus, a certain amount of time would have elapsed giving time for second thoughts. With e-mail the message is on the composer's screen one moment and on the recipient's screen the next – there is little thinking or reflection time.

Case study 13.3

COME BACK MESSAGE, ALL IS FORGIVEN

The agent had just received a surface mail letter from a landlord which seemed to indicate that they thought he was acting without instructions. As it was the second time this had occurred he was somewhat annoyed and seeing that there was an e-mail address available immediately sent a message which in essence accused the landlord of deliberately being obtuse in order to slow down the negotiations, but making it appear that he was at fault.

Within minutes an equally angry retort had appeared on his screen completely denying all knowledge of the accusation and suggesting that he re-read the latest letter. This he did and realised that his initial under-standing was not borne out by the contents.

Key technique

Had the complaint been lodged by a telephone call there might have been some mileage in trying to convince the other side that it was a misunderstanding. However, using e-mail gave both the instant reaction and the permanent copy of the complaint – no matter how ill-founded.

Warning: It should not be overlooked that whilst it may be possible to comment on third parties over the phone and even to slander them with little chance of retribution, since seldom does a permanent record exist of the call, if such comments are put in writing – as they can be via e-mail – then not only does slander become the more serious wrong of libel, but also a permanent record of such comments exists and may come back to haunt the originator.

211

Softening the words

The real trouble is the words we use may not have the same meaning to those who read them. Perhaps a couple of examples may highlight this point which should be obvious and yet is often totally overlooked.

Case study

DANGER – MISCOMMUNICATION AT WORK (1)

The following memo was sent out by one of the UK's companies to a number of subscribers to a directory that it produced:

'A spot check of randomly selected directories indicates that a number of such directories contain several blank pages. In view of the foregoing it is suggested that each user review his or her directory and ascertain whether or not the directory contains blank pages. In the event that this is the case and the directory is incomplete, the user should return the directory to source for disposition.'

We will ignore the fact that the message would have been far more effective if the author had said

'Please check your directory. If it contains any blank pages send it to me with your name and address and I'll replace it'

which would not only have been easier to understand, but also would have told those with incomplete directories how to go about getting a complete directory – a vital fact that the original version does not address! What is more relevant is that when shown this delightful farrago of jargon, some readers commented

'What case do they mean?'

'Why are they talking about sauce?'

'What does disposition mean?'

If the reader does not understand the message it is the writer's fault and responsibility. It is interesting to note that the babbling of an infant (which word itself comes from the Latin 'infans' meaning 'without words') is called 'jargon' – a meaningless noise. Those who use jargon should be warned accordingly – who knows, it might even cure them!

Case study

DANGER – MISCOMMUNICATION AT WORK (2)

The following notice appears in the entrance of a sports centre

'Please to be advised that you are now entering a facility where smoking is not permitted other than in the confines of the bar.'

When invited to come in for a drink, one person replied that they had no wish to use a cramped bar for a drink – mistaking 'confines' for 'confined'. The message *'no smoking please – other than in the bar'* would have been a far clearer message and one that would be less open to misunderstanding.

Warning: Using high flown language and verbosity actually impresses few people – probably only the impressionable who, with all due respect, are hardly a great audience to satisfy. Equally it is important neither to underestimate intelligence nor to overestimate knowledge. Most people are quite capable of understanding the most complex information provided it is explained in language with which they are familiar and without jargon. Failure to credit people with intelligence is infuriating to them and can create barriers impeding the route to understanding.

Jargon has been defined – and decried – earlier in this book and should always be avoided.

Bearing in mind the references to the virtual office, surfing the Internet and the rapid technological advances it is perhaps appropriate to refer to George Orwell. In his (then) futuristic novel '1984', Orwell invented the land of totalitarianism ruled by the all-seeing dictator, Big Brother, where to try to contain or remove dissident thought, the language, 'Newspeak', was reduced to very few words. Whilst, as far as its actual intent, such a concept is impossible (most languages in use tend to expand by a small proportion each year) the theory of using fewer rather than more words in certain contexts is sound. Away from the nightmarish '1984', Orwell developed a number of guidelines for good use of English including those set out below.

213

Guidelines to written language

- Avoid using a metaphor or simile or other figure of speech which you are used to seeing in print
  (We could add 'never mix a metaphor' since if you do you may find there are a lot of hiccups to be ironed out. Very nasty!)

- Use short words rather than long words

- Avoid verbosity – cut out redundant words
  (Authors of Sports Centre notices please note.)

- Never use jargon, or scientific or foreign words if you can use ordinary everyday English words
  (Authors of memos *re* faulty directories please note.)

- Always use the active tense rather than the passive
  and above all

- Break any or all of these guidelines rather than say anything that is outright barbarous!

(From *Politics and the English language* by George Orwell)

Once we deviate from guidelines like these, we can become trapped in a 'Newspeak' of our own, where the words constantly get in the way of the meaning.

Games people play

In sending e-mail messages because the novelty of the process is almost like playing, senders can be deluded into taking a casual approach to their task. Graham Marriner, Strategy Manager at the Post Office, commented,

'you often get people's immediate thoughts . . . people just dash off messages and typically don't read them back or check what they have said – they just press the send button and it's gone. A day later the recipient might come on the phone upset about something in the message and the sender is completely mystified.'

Case study 13.4

'CAR ON WHERE WE LEFT'

'Post lunch to Derby. Visitors then car to unit 3. Review updated procedures and products and sample lines.'

Key technique

The casual approach to e-mail also tends to trap unwary users into a kind of cartoon-like truncated language where nouns are used as verbs and, if we are not careful, sense can be lost rather than relayed. Here one could be forgiven for querying why the recipient has to send their sandwiches to the Midlands whilst using the noun 'car' as a verb (ie the meaning is the visitors will be transported by car to unit 3) raises the additional query – am I supposed to make sure the visitor's car is moved to unit 3 or am I supposed to carry the visitors to unit 3?

This extract from a message concerning a visit of Japanese visitors (who tend to be smaller than Europeans which could reassure the reader if they are to be carried!) indicates that the visitors will travel by car to the next factory where not only will they be able to inspect the modernised production process but also will be able to sample the latest products. If that is what is meant why not say so – it only takes 33 words at maximum against 17 and how long does it take to type 16 words? Less time certainly than to explain to a puzzled recipient what the message actually means.

Danger ahead

Whilst there is an obviously funny side to this, there can also be very serious consequences should the wrong person read our message – particularly if we have dashed it off with little thought. There has already been one libel action brought concerning a libel via the Internet (the case, between two scientists was settled out of court in mid-1995) and one libel case concerning alleged defamation via the contents of internal e-mail messages (the *Western Provident v Norwich Union* case which awaits resolution as this book goes to press). It is understood that the whole question of libel *via* e-mail and the Internet is to be considered for legislation in the UK during 1996–97.

Meet the smilies

Unintentional insults, mistakes or misunderstandings can be offset to a limited extent by using a new language – the smilies. Communication via e-mail is essentially based around the traditional typewriter keyboard but using the 100 or so characters and letters available can and has created a number of tiny cartoon messages which many devotees of e-mail now incorporate in their messages (see box overleaf). If you like they are the equivalent of some of the body language that both phone and e-mail lack. You need to turn the book through 90° to see the effect.

David Sanderson, who the *Wall Street Journal* refers to as 'the Noah Webster of Smilies' has collected around 600 of these symbols. Whilst some may be very obscure, as they come more into use, they should help us understand what was the intended meaning of the writer which we cannot gain simply from the words. Indeed they should not be dismissed as idle fun – if they become widely used on an international scale we may well find in the 21st century that we do at last have an international language – using not words but symbols. Bearing in mind the oft-repeated phrase that a picture is worth 1,000 words, these little cartoon char-

Smiley and Co (some old and some new devices to tone down or up electronically transmitted messages).

:-)	The original 'smiley' used to indicate a joke or pleasantry or that the words are not meant to be taken too literally
(-:	This is a version of the smiley for those who are left handed
.-)	The winkie – indicating that it's an aside, again not to be taken too literally
:-(	Sad or unhappy
:- ‖	Signifies anger (an emotion which is one of the easiest to indicate in writing)
:-{	I have a moustache (possibly of use during the exchange between the two librarians referred to above)
:-#	Kiss (no doubt also used by the librarians)
:-?	I am smoking . . . a pipe
:-i	. . . or a cigarette
:-'(	I have a cold
:"-(	I'm in tears
:^)	That's put *his/her* nose out of joint
(:-)	Baldheaded
:-O	Yawn yawn
:-/	Undecided
:-‖ :-‖	Two-faced
:-Y	Speaks with forked tongue
:-x	Keep your mouth shut

Warning: Capitals are little used in e-mail. If you do use capitals for the message or part of it, it is usually taken to mean either that you are shouting or you are angry. Regardless of this semiotic message, text in capitals should be avoided as, back to basics again, it tends to be difficult to read.

acters may be the forerunner of a language that not only has international acceptance but also general comprehension of meaning *in the way that the writer intended* – which might be the first time any human language has achieved that.

It is not only in communication via computer that such devices are used. The City University Business School in its booklet *Improving the communication of accounting information* records that stylised human faces in a variety of expressions are being used to give readers a fast insight into a company's accounts. The faces are based on liquidity (angle of the eyebrow), working capital (length and width of nose), financial leverage (eye size and eyebrow length) and profitability (mouth curve, length and eye pupil position. Author of the report Professor Richard Tafler commented 'Psychological studies show that we assimilate visual stimuli much more quickly than either verbal or quantitative information'. Tests have disclosed that use of the faces cut by over 50 per cent the time taken to absorb accounts and ratios and helped reduce analysis errors.

Messages in traditional languages tend to mean different things despite the most careful endeavour. This has been noticed in the advertising world where trying to roll out an acceptable and known phrase can have unfortunate consequences. Apparently Pepsi Cola's phrase 'come alive with Pepsi' was translated into an Asiatic language as 'Pepsi brings your ancestors back from the dead'; Kentucky Fried Chicken's 'finger-lickin' good' was translated into Chinese as 'eat your fingers off' and washing powder ads that showed the three stages of washing – 'dirty', 'dirty plus powder', 'clean' – forgot that in many languages the message is read from right to left. The question of transmitting messages to e-mail readers who read from right to left and from the foot of the page to the top poses a problem – capable of solution but one can only provide a solution when the question has been identified. Symbols may help – colours, which also have messages of their own, may not.

The sting in the tail
■ ■ ■

Each year in the UK there are around 25 billion business calls made – 20 billion from business numbers plus up to a further 5 billion from private numbers which are being used to run businesses in and from their owners' homes. This is a figure which must grow as teleworking itself grows. If we believe estimates that around 10 million people use the Internet each day and over 80 per cent are using it for e-mail that amounts to around 8 million such messages each day – say a further 3 billion a year and growing rapidly.

In considering the toughness of business calls, the research referred to previously which indicates that only 11 per cent of the message being conveyed is retained, bears repeating. In using the phone for many instances where we need our message to get through it might be advisable to bear in mind the old advice concerning training – 'You need to tell 'em you're going to tell 'em, tell 'em and tell 'em you've told 'em'. This is our communication challenge.

The rapidly changing technological advances mean that fewer 'foot soldiers', that is the unskilled or those with a low level of skills, are needed. Following extensive research, leading consultants McKinsey estimate that by the year 2000, 70 per cent of all European jobs will require professional skills (that is 'A' level or higher) whilst the remaining 30 per cent will require skills only marginally less. The Confederation of British Industry, commenting on this research, stressed that 'outstanding communication skills' will be needed by these employees. Equally outstanding communication skills will be needed in order to deal with them. **For every manager, indeed every person required to interface with another, there is an urgent need to hone and improve their communication skills.** If this is essential in terms of face to face communication it is absolutely vital when we are not physically present with the target for our messages.

If we can only solve the problem when we understand the question, perhaps the main problem is that, because it is instinctive, human communication tends to be taken for granted and we assume that because we know what we mean, the other party will understand. Regardless of what method of communication we are using, this is a mighty big assumption – and in most cases will be entirely false. Starting from another assumption – that we cannot assume that the other side will understand our real meaning – may be invaluable. Simple human communication may turn out to be the greatest challenge of the 21st century. We certainly have the technology and every technological assistance, but the constant question we need to ask ourselves is do we understand what we are trying to communicate and, more importantly, will our target?

219

Appendix

■ ■ ■

100 practical pointers – a handy guide to tactics and devices

Ten basics to consider before we start

1 A telephone (and/or an e-mail screen) should be regarded with caution not casual familiarity. They are devices for communication made between two persons separated by mutual misconceptions and prejudices.

2 This problem can be exacerbated when we are trying to interface with a person from a different culture, using a different language and attitude and lacking the advantage of them being able to see our body language (and we theirs).

3 If the listener does not understand the message it is not their fault – the responsibility lies with the originator.

4 The telephone is the thought interrupter *par excellence* – as such, despite the innocuous nature of the call, it may provoke irritation from the recipient.

5 Callers should not be kept hanging on – unless you want to create a tough call.

6 If you have a position where you are required to answer queries it is essential that all the information to deal with these is available to you – and immediately adjacent to the work station on which you are taking/making the call or contact.

7 Standard procedures are fine provided they are only used for standard questions/problems. Using a standard response for a non-standard question can only create or worsen tough calls.

8 Be prepared. Being unable to answer a simple query creates irritation and hardly reflects well on the organisation – or your own expertise.

9 Never (never, never, never, never) lose your temper (unless done deliberately for effect) or use sarcasm. The effect will usually be to create a similar response in the other party. 'He who loses his temper, loses the argument.'

10 Don't assume that a call (and its outcome) will remain confidential between the parties. If one party has been unfairly bested by the other, he or she will almost certainly talk to others about their treatment. If this is a customer the ripples can spread widely.

Ten ideal actions and attributes

1 To be able to think quickly (as well as laterally or innovatively).

2 To train ourselves to listen very carefully to the message actually being said (not the one we think is being said).

3 To be ready whenever we pick up the phone (whether making or taking) for the dynamic interplay we may then face.

4 To record what you think you have been asked on the telephone, in writing (preferably also asking for confirmation).

5 To remember SARAH – **S**mile and stop talking, **A**ctively listen, **R**epeat the content, **A**ct with empathy, **H**andle the subject matter with an appreciation of the feelings of the other side.

6 To respect the need for the recipient to defer dealing with the call and be prepared to wait.

7 To ensure the recipient is the right person to deal with the call you are making.

8 To have the paperwork ready when making a calling; get it when taking a call – facts provide valuable defences and weapons.

9 Before making any tough call to make a comprehensive list of all the factors and facts bearing on the matter and all the items that need to be considered.

10 To be assertive. Everyone has the right to put their views forward and have them listened to, to disagree with others and to consider where we are and where we go from here.

Ten problems to guard against

1 Those used to power and exercising it will try to roll over the recipient – defensive tactics to halt this steamroller effect are essential.

2 Callers make calls at times convenient to themselves – if it is inconvenient arrange to ring them back (but make sure you do).

3 Because we are committed to a course of action or particular scenario we need to guard against assuming others will see things the same way. (Assume makes an 'ass' of 'u' and 'me'. We cannot afford to assume, we need to find out. Assumptions tend to make arguments.)

4 Because we are enthusiastic about a course of action/product/ service we may be trapped into assuming that we know everything about the recipient's need for this item. We won't, but inferring we do may create a tough call.

5 No two person's requirements are the same – neither are any two calls – we need to treat each as a fresh challenge. We may be able to amend previous tactics but should not simply re-use them without appreciating the different situations.

6 If we initiate a call our attitude may well condition a similar attitude in the recipient – anger tends to create anger, laughter to create relaxation, etc.

7 Some callers plan their whole conversation, constructing questions that force answers from the recipient so that the conversation is guided to its predetermined conclusion. This kind of call must be recognised, guarded against and the flow broken to avoid being manipulated.

8 Reflection may suggest that there was a better way of dealing with some calls. This means that decisions were taken without sufficient time being allowed for considerations of alternative responses. Don't be afraid to break the flow and state that you want to think things over.

9 If being required to deal with the media, whose interest in the subject matter tends to have a lower priority than their need to fill column inches and/or air time, and who may be prepared to make up 'facts' if they cannot obtain them, adequate preparation, training and briefing is essential.

223

10 Adopting a proactive attitude when things are quiet may assist phoning and briefing the media when there is a crisis (when time tends to be at a premium).

Ten ways to achieve short effective calls

1 Know who you need to talk to.

2 Know what it is you need to say/discover.

3 Keep preliminaries and pleasantries to a minimum. (eg 'I realise how busy you are so I don't want to take up too much of your time' is a clever ploy to shorten a call. Few will wish to admit that they are not busy!)

4 Be brief – brief questions, brief answers, brief comments.

5 Make the call – don't take it. If you make the first move you hold the initiative and should be able to control the length.

6 Check if the time is convenient. If not, arrange a time that is, don't say 'I'll call back later' – say when.

7 Listen carefully to what is said, make notes and check if there is anything of which you are unclear ('Can I just check I've got that right . . .')

8 Speak quickly but clearly and try to avoid being interrupted ('Could you excuse me for a second whilst I put this point across . . .')

9 Make notes of what was said and agreed in order to avoid having to ring back to check points.

10 If necessary recap of what has been agreed.

Ten pointers to aid customer care

1 Provide a freephone number if customers are required to ring with complaints and may be kept hanging on.

2 Avoid putting callers in the transfer call cycle where the only way they can stop the automatic process is by ringing off and starting again. Inserting a human voice or answerphone into the cycle should help avoid creating tough calls.

3 Set up systems (and man them) so that no-one waits more than 20 seconds.

4 When a caller has been kept waiting the first action should be to apologise.

5 Use DARN (**D**iscovery, **A**pology, **R**ectification and **N**ovation) is a sound watchword for dealing with tough calls and avoiding their future incidence.

6 Carelines and helplines can defuse tough calls.

7 Customers', complaining calls can be defused to some extent by owning the problem and dealing with it promptly – this can also convert a complainer into a fan.

8 Dealing with problems and complaints swiftly (KISS – **K**eep **I**t **S**imple **S**tupid) is essential to reduce the effect and incidence of tough calls.

9 'If you can fake sincerity – you have got it made.' A sincere reaction will help avoid or defuse tough calls.

225

10 After a difficult or argumentative call make notes of what went wrong and try to analyse what it was.

Ten aids to getting what you want

1 Determine your desired result and always have it in mind.

2 Make a list of everything you want – and what you are prepared to give in order to achieve it.

3 Make a list of fall back positions – and of the absolute minimum you require.

4 Consider what the other party will want and whether there is any way in which by giving them part or all, in order to help achieve your aim.

5 Ensure the party you are ringing is capable of giving you what you want – if not try and arrange to contact someone who can.

6 Encourage the other party to speak and put their points (even if you do not agree with them ('yes', 'I see', 'Mmmm', 'that's interesting') are all ways of encouraging the other party to speak

without commitment on your part. The more a person speaks the more they tend to reveal of their 'case' and commitment to it).

7 Try to determine reasons why you cannot agree with their comments – not simply dismissing them out of hand.

8 Giving way on some minor points may enable you to win on the more major points.

9 Remember your scale of fall backs, but try only to fall back one step at a time.

10 Each time you fall back try to win something for the concession.

Ten aspects for aiding or defending cold calling

1 Preparation is essential. Discover the name of the target, appreciate and anticipate their negative (even hostile) reaction, find an edge to gain their attention, find a peg on which you can hang their interest.

2 Treat junior people with respect and as human beings to gain an entrée to their office (and boss).

3 Devise something with originality to counter the instinctive lack of interest. Arouse the curiosity.

4 After a successful call similarly analyse why it was successful and remember it in case it can be of use in the future.

5 Devise and practise 'continuous closing sentences' to bring cold calls to a swift end.

6 Recognise the different types of cold callers and be ready with the appropriate close down tactic.

7 Have the responses typed out and kept in readiness by the phone.

8 Practise speaking the responses so that there is a familiarity in their use.

9 Brief others who may take your calls with the same tactics.

10 If there was any particular device, comment or counter (whether used by or against you) that seemed to be particularly effective, make a note of it for the future.

Ten points for closing down unwanted calls

1 'That's very interesting but I have no time to consider it just now – drop me a line about it and if it is appropriate I will call you.' This returns control to you.

2 'It is not our policy to buy in response to cold calls – please put details in writing and we may consider them at the appropriate time.' Returns control without any commitment.

3 'No, we've considered this idea before and we are not interested.'

4 'That idea is not appropriate to our line of business.'

5 'We are in the middle of a reorganisation and the timing is totally wrong. Please drop us a line in about six months' time.'

6 'The person you need to speak to is away for x weeks but I can confirm that my knowledge of the situation indicates that that is inappropriate for us.'

7 'We have a number of changes to implement and it would not be feasible to consider anything further.'

8 Avoid any suggestion that you should debate the matter. 'We do not discuss such matters over the phone.'

9 If there is a reply to '8' simply say '10'.

10 To all of the above add 'Thank you for calling' and replace the receiver in one fluid movement allowing no space for any interjections.

227

Ten points for gaining control

1 Prepare, prepare, prepare.

2 Have all the facts, data, records at your fingertips.

3 Use a précis so that whatever item you need it is instantly available thus avoiding delay, hesitation, etc.

4 Know the fall back positions and get authority to use them.

5 Resist pressure by relying on the facts.

6 Use a loudspeaker phone.

7 Move around whilst talking if it makes you feel less inhibited when dealing with a tough call.

8 Don't try to deal with a call unless you are prepared – arrange to ring back (not only will this give you time to prepare but also you will gain a slight edge by making rather than taking the call).

9 If the call is likely to be tough – consider all that can be thrown at you and prepare appropriate defences. Not only will this aid the information flow, but also you will feel more confident about handling the call.

10 Lock the door so that you can concentrate on dealing with the call – interruptions distract attention, ruin concentration and may reduce confidence.

Ten points about the new technology

228

1 Answerphones are very useful but leaving messages needs careful thought – it's a permanent message of your comments.

2 Like making a telephone call or leaving an e-mail message, often we do not prepare ourselves to talk to a machine and leave a poor message or, if angry, one that may not be strictly true. It may be better to hang up – prepare what we want to say and then ring back.

3 Even though we have a valid case, the recipient can destroy it by concentrating on any exaggeration or false comment of which a permanent taped record exists. The validity of the remainder of the message can be ignored.

4 It may be helpful to use an answerphone to monitor calls. Listening to the caller leaving a message provides time to think of a response – either for immediate or later use.

5 The Internet (or even an internal linked computer system) provides a superb means of swift communication. It is essential to think before we use it to ensure the message we wish to send is framed in a way that the recipient will understand it in the way we wish.

6 The barriers to communication (see Chapter Two) apply in their own way to the use of e-mail and we need to ensure we do

as much as possible to minimise these barriers. Messages should be prepared and time for consideration provided before they are sent.

7 Careless choice of words can mean that we create problems where none existed. If used on the phone we may be able to explain the mistake away as a slip of the tongue, but if the words are transmitted via e-mail they have a permanence which can rebound on us.

8 Messages should be kept short – but not so short that essential meaning is lost or confusion is created.

9 Symbols (internationally recognised) may help both to informalise or personalise messages (removing the stiffness created by the words without body language) and may provide the means by which there is a greater understanding of meaning.

10 The growth of teleworking inevitably means that the use of both phone and e-mail will increase dramatically. To use both we need to prepare and improve our language skills. In using both mediums our body language is not available to provide 40 per cent of the message transmission that we can use in face to face communication.

Index

■ ■ ■